FOOT LOOSE

Charlie Smith's Offshore Chronicles

Third Edition

Fred Sharp

 **www.trafford.com**

North America & international
toll-free: 1 888 232 4444 (USA & Canada)
phone: 250 383 6864 ♦ fax: 250 383 6804 ♦ email: info@trafford.com

The United Kingdom & Europe
phone: +44 (0)1865 722 113 ♦ local rate: 0845 230 9601
facsimile: +44 (0)1865 722 868 ♦ email: info.uk@trafford.com

20 19 18 17 16 15 14 13 12 11

To my wife Teresa,

and to my children
Alexander and Natalie

Who lighten my life daily.

Preface to the Third Edition

Since the First Edition was published in 2003, the offshore world has been buffeted by change, and has adapted.

The legacy of the big governments' recent pressure is a seismic shift away from illegitimate and politically-incorrect business. No longer will the offshore jurisdictions harbor fugitives or their ill-gotten gains. Not only are drug dealers out, but also tax-evaders, fraudsters and other white collar criminals. Obviously there are some scalawags who slip through the nets, but their former havens have recognized they can no longer afford to snub their big brothers. They have learned how power can be focused, like a magnifying glass in sunlight. Today those scoundrels, once in, must keep a lower profile than they did at home!

As the targets continue to multiply, the offshore jurisdictions continue to refine their services. Two new targets are terrorism and stock market manipulation, which present serious challenges to the banking industry everywhere. Trying to police international banking flies in the face of globalization. How this will develop in the near future is anyone's guess.

All this is made possible, of course, by computerization. For the first time, governments can track, store, retrieve, analyze and deploy the data necessary to ascertain trends, gather evidence and pursue their quarry. Digitization makes this process efficient, inexpensive and remarkably effective. Working together, they can now pool their resources. It is becoming impossible to hide anywhere.

So here we are, living in fast-paced, complex societies full of contradictions and traps, being forced to hide in plain view, but hide nevertheless to protect privacy and property from those who would be obeyed. The new freedom appears to be an ever-narrowing path towards what is good for you and away from the bad, as determined by your government. Is the second great lie being forgotten?

As the globe inches its way towards centralized rule, the offshore world continues to play a pivotal role, albeit hiding those with nothing to hide.

Fred Sharp
September, 2007

Forward

Charlie Smith came to Offshore Finance Canada Magazine courtesy of his creator and chronicler, Fred Sharp, with an idea. He wanted to bring the common man's perspective to the myriad aspects of offshore life which we were writing about. Thus Charlie Smith's Offshore Chronicles began, as a feature in Offshore Finance Canada Magazine, focussing on the world of offshore business, finance and investment. The first article (which is chapter one in this book) appeared in the July, 1999 issue, and was an immediate success.

Blessed with a rapier "sharp" wit and a keen flair for storytelling, Fred makes insightful comments on the state of offshore finance through Charlie. The fifty-something Charlie has been through a lot, as he tries his best to stay one step ahead of the taxman and overzealous government bodies. It's been a roller-coaster ride for poor old Charlie, to say the least. But it's a ride we've all enjoyed.

And now, fans of Charlie can follow all of his adventures in Fred's wildly entertaining new book. Each of the chapters bears the date of its original publication as a reference point, since many dealt with events that occurred at those times. Readers will no doubt recognize Fred's cleverly veiled references to some of the major issues facing the offshore finance industry today: the Organization for Economic Cooperation and Development's so-called Harmful Tax Practices campaign, the Financial Task Force's anti-money laundering blacklist, and so on.

This book has the added bonus of Fred's fanciful sketches,

which appear here for the first time. Now we know what Charlie looks like, as he meanders his way from place to place, seeking his fortune while avoiding fame.

As long as there is an offshore world, Charlie will be there, exploiting the opportunities that come his way. We are sure you will enjoy reading these Chronicles as much as our readers have over the years.

Brian Stammer, Publisher
Offshore Finance Canada Magazine
January, 2003

Table of Contents

Introduction

*"Above all a prince should abstain from the property of others,
because men sooner forget the death of their father
than the loss of their inheritance."*

— Machiavelli

There is a little of Charlie Smith in all of us, full of hopes and desires as he tries to get ahead. Like us, he is surrounded by good people and some not so good, who influence his life. Unlike some of us, he is constantly buffeted by events beyond his control, often with unpredictable results.

Charlie is not always successful in his plans. Sometimes he fails completely, but he always manages to adapt and bounce back. Nor is he perfect, frequently succumbing to temptations that would make some blush.

In other words, Charlie Smith is human, bringing his unique attitudes to each circumstance that confronts him. As his chronicler, I have embellished his adventures to emphasize the pertinent legal and philosophical issues. With this introduction, I would like to highlight those issues, since they form the basis of the stories that follow.

What is Offshore?

In essence, the offshore world is about people and assets:

those with assets which they want to move, protect and invest; those who want to control those assets; and still others who help them move, protect and invest their assets.

This vibrant field of human endeavor, as Charlie Smith demonstrates, is both rooted in human nature and characterized by human ingenuity.

People by nature work hardest when they work for themselves. From this work ethic springs a natural desire to hold onto the fruits of our labor, which emotionally groups tax collectors with thieves, con men, used car salesmen and others who try to part us from our money without giving fair value in return.

Some of us might even wish to see bureaucrats "skewered through and through with office pens, and bound hand and foot with red tape" as Charles Dickens recommended in *David Copperfield.*

Whatever the sentiment, people are inclined to accumulate assets as a defense against the vagaries of their uncertain lives. In a world where social status still derives from wealth, it cannot be expected that the desire to preserve that wealth will soon disappear.

Until that day comes, an inevitable conflict with those who would lighten our purses will continue, skewered or not.

What is Onshore?

Against this backdrop of natural desire we are witness to increasingly complex laws and technologies designed to tax, fine, confiscate and otherwise redistribute our assets. These products of the ingenuity of politicians and bureaucrats in turn lead to equally ingenious counter-measures designed to shield their targets.

Depending on your point of view, the terms to describe government intrusion range from taxation and protection of the public to theft and legalized oppression. Likewise, the terms for moving, protecting and investing assets range from tax planning, privacy and asset protection to tax evasion, money laundering and treason.

This is heady stuff, caused principally by the voracious appetite of governments for cash to fund their social programs and their highly publicized causes. With the explosion of computerization, governments have the tools to eliminate privacy within their borders; conversely, individuals increasingly have the ability to regain that lost privacy offshore.

In a very real sense, the offshore world reflects the age-old conflict between the interests of the state and those of the individual. While we are predisposed to support the fight against drugs and terrorism, it is much harder to endorse erroneous attacks on innocent people, no matter how lawful.

While we accept taxation as necessary to provide us with the many benefits of collective living, many continue to question the complex ways governments squander the extra money they do not appear to need.

While we recognize the argument for some government regulation to modulate human activity, we resent the excessive bureaucratic red tape that inevitably seems to result. Office pens anyone?

At the end of the day, when accosted by men in brown suits who tell us they are here to help us by taking much of our property for the greater social good, do we, can we wholeheartedly believe them?

We may comply, however grudgingly, partly because we are members of societies that expect and need our support in exchange for the protection they provide us, and failure to do so is contrary to law and incurs stiff penalties.

From the beginning of recorded thought, philosophers have sought that elusive grail of the ideal social contract where citizens live together in harmony governed by fair and enlightened rulers.

This social contract creates philosophical and ethical dimensions for offshore considerations: what is the proper balance between powers and liberties in a just society; when is civil disobedience justified; what rights to privacy and property do citizens have; what level of government intrusion and taxation is fair; is it right to move, protect and invest assets?

The purpose of governments is to provide for their citizens. They raise taxes to pay for the services they provide (or at least that is the theory). Consequently the offshore world has been given a bad rap by those who feel threatened by its competition.

To those who oppose international planning, one might ask: is it fair to tax people on their worldwide incomes when they do not live in one country all year long? Should not taxes be in line with the caliber of services that government provides?

As life becomes more global and electronic, mobility is on the rise. This is in direct opposition to income tax, which assumes we will stay in one place.

Since every society is a collective of people who associate in order to enjoy common benefits, the answers to these questions can be found in the will and expectations of each citizen.

Where is Offshore?

It is here that the offshore world begins, with individuals who, for numerous reasons, want or need an alternative location to their home countries for themselves, their assets, or both. There is nothing new under the sun about this world, for people have sought to protect themselves and their property since the dawn of man.

Throughout history there have been looters and pillagers, monarchs, dictators and pirates from whom people have had to protect their property. Motivated by self-preservation, they have sought, found and created alternatives to exposing their assets, from which we have inherited the offshore corporation, asset protection trust, private foundation, and the famous numbered Swiss bank account.

A traditional rivalry has evolved between the chasers and the chased, posing the recurring question of who are the real "hoodlums" in the chase.

One early-day tax exile was none other than the legendary Robin Hood, perhaps the foremost social worker in England. Hiding out in Sherwood Forest, robbing from the rich and giving to the poor, he has come to represent the dire straits of the oppressed under Prince John in the late twelfth century, and the rebellion against high taxes and abuse of power.

With his merry band, Robin led the fight against the government and the church, executing a limited but significant wealth redistribution plan. Communication and transportation being slow and arduous, they chose nearby Sherwood Forest as their international financial center where they could remove their private affairs from prying eyes. The deep woods provided ample asset protection and secrecy.

Viewed from this perspective, going offshore can be called "voting with your feet", or as I prefer to think of it, taking matters into our own hands which are best not left to others, be they governments or creditors.

By now you will have a good idea of how the word "offshore"

is used in this book. It is a term based on contrast. Onshore is where you live, and offshore is anywhere else that has laws and investment incentives which better suit your needs.

The offshore states have on their side history, philosophy and psychology in their resistance to the pursuit of a world dominated by a big brother and his thought police who know what is best for their citizens.

People onshore have discovered the offshore world in a serious way, and are increasingly discontent with government strategies which abridge their freedoms in the pursuit of fair taxation.

Charlie Smith's World

Welcome then to Charlie's offshore world, where fragrant breezes gently rustle palm leaves which shade exotic drinks sporting little paper umbrellas. Where pristine beaches meet azure blue seas. Where office pens are but a memory, and skewers reserved for barbequing tropical dishes.

Where pirates once plied their trade and now sophisticated professionals handle trillions of dollars of assets for a global clientele. Where everyone is welcome, provided they have the proper references and can establish a clean financial pedigree.

Where there is an exciting and vital life dedicated to enhancing wealth and protecting privacy. It is a world driven by individuality, and one that would have appealed to Robin Hood and his compatriots.

1.

Lost Ground to the Underground Economy

July, 1999

"The internal revenue service has made more liars out of U.S. persons than golf."

— Will Rogers

Charlie Smith was worried. The income tax men were going to visit him tomorrow about his tax returns. Something about earnings and his lifestyle. He did not quite understood what it was all about as he reassured the investigator that his books were in order. Of course he was happy to oblige, he said. Tomorrow at 9:30 in the morning? No problem, he said.

A short, balding man in his mid-fifties, Charlie had transplanted himself years earlier from the East end of London to a land of greater opportunity. Always one to stretch a dollar, he also decided to reduce his tax burden. He preferred to think of it as a proactive tax reduction strategy.

Charlie could do this, he reasoned, by not declaring 60% of the cash income from his vending machine business. This would bring his tax obligation in line with what he should be paying. Since everyone was doing it, how much trouble could he get into?

At first it was a simple matter to roll the coins and stack them in the closet in his basement office. But coins are bulky, and over time he ran out of space. Not only this, but the remaining 40% was not enough to cover the costs of his lifestyle, which were considerable, and growing, since he had a penchant for the finer things.

It also irked him to think of all that cash sitting in the closet not earning interest. Charlie had no choice but to approach the problem methodically.

First Step: the Local Bank

Bundling some of the coins into one of those large black brief cases that trial lawyers use, he wrenched his arm as he muscled it into his vintage Mercedes. He drove to his bank, where he was confronted by stone steps separating him from the doors.

Some effort later, Charlie entered the bank, only to find it packed with customers quietly waiting for the next available teller.

When his turn finally came in the queue, he dragged his case up to the teller and presented his deposit slip for $12,480.

At this point he encountered two problems: the large number of coins had to be special handled at the side counter, and there was a form that needed to be filled out to disclose the source of this money, since it was over $10,000.

Charlie looked at the form, and tried to maintain his composure as sheer panic started to course through his veins. Nervously thanking the teller, be pulled the case over to the counter.

When he was certain the teller was busy with another customer, Charlie skulked out of the bank hoping no one would remember, or worse, record his visit.

"What will you do now, my lad?" he said to himself in the privacy of his car, the coins safely stashed back in the trunk. Then he had a good idea: he would take the coins to one of those exchange places where people buy and sell gold bars. There was one a few blocks away.

Next Step: the Local Exchange

Twenty minutes later, he was sitting before a clerk pouring over the price list of gold coins, wafers and bars.

"Must I fill out one of those horrid forms about my coins if I decide to buy some of these gold wafers?" he asked.

"Certainly not sir," came the welcome reply.

"Very well," Charlie said. "I should be much obliged if you would sell me eighty-three of these small wafers." Whereupon the clerk produced an exchange contract and began to fill it in.

"Now sir, may I please see your driver's license." The now too familiar feeling of panic returned as Charlie shifted uneasily in his chair. His mind raced.

Regaining his composure, Charlie delicately asked: "Forgive me for asking, you see I'm new at this, but why do you need my driver's license?"

"As a regulated bullion dealer, we must record every gold trade," said the clerk. "It's the law, and it's also for your protection in case the gold is lost or stolen."

"I see," Charlie replied weakly. "Perhaps I will wait a day or two," he said as he retreated to his car, bag in tow, for the second time.

Crestfallen, Charlie returned home, poured himself a double scotch on the rocks and pondered his predicament. There was no other solution: he would just have to take the next step.

Charlie reasoned he could establish accounts at a variety of banks and other financial institutions – say ten to start with – where he could exchange his coins for cash in varying amounts under $10,000. Then he could use that cash to pay for as many goods and services as possible.

Dinners out were an especially good choice, since he could still write off the expense receipts.

Charlie had read the newspaper reports about the underground economy, about how alarming numbers of people were evading taxes by paying cash. If they could do it, well, he had to be as smart as they were.

He had to think harder. Paying for repairs to his house with cash was a thought. Maybe he should add a new room with a walk-in safe to hold the cash.

Stepping Up

And so it happened that through the years Charlie Smith discovered more and more outlets for his cash. His business grew, which meant he had ever more coins, and therefore cash, to fuel his increasingly lavish lifestyle.

He built a bigger house (which had a walk-in safe hidden in the basement) in a better neighborhood. He bought a newer car (he tried to pay cash but he ran into the old disclosure problem; he was told it was something about money laundering which the salesman assured him certainly had nothing to do with him).

He even kept an apartment in town where he could stay when he did not feel like going home. His was the life of Riley, he mused to himself – the perfect crime.

Except that two investigators from the tax department were coming to see him tomorrow morning. They had even suggested it would be in his best interest to cooperate. He was not sure why the person on the phone had been so reproachful. After all, he was not a criminal.

If he had done anything at all, it was only to modulate the amount of taxes he paid each year. Taxes which in everyone's opinion were way too high.

The Audit

Tomorrow came and went in the typical fashion of a tax audit. The investigators arrived armed with bank statements obtained from many of his various accounts, past filings and the like. They took great interest in his grand house and its décor. Charlie was almost flattered as he showed them his rich art collection on the way down to the den. They all sat down at his period desk, a few yards from the hidden safe.

Harold Wong, the more senior auditor, explained the consequences of tax evasion, and warned Charlie to come clean. The younger auditor said very little, but his steely gray eyes said it all: "We've got you – hook, line and sinker. Don't deny it, or it will only go harder on you." Those eyes seemed to see right through him.

At length, a negotiation of sorts occurred; one-sided of course as tax audits invariably are. Not only did they have enough to put him away, as Wong so indelicately put it, but everything he prized would be lost to pay the tax bill.

They had everything they needed: names, dates, amounts, the works. Charlie was despondent.

Then the unexpected happened. Wong said the department was prepared to accept its calculation of the taxes owed plus interest, without any penalties, in full settlement of the claim.

Charlie did a quick calculation, and realized that, all in, he was still slightly ahead. He'd have to go straight, of course. Well, more or less straight. He agreed, and signed the paper.

Aftermath

As they were leaving the bigger house in the better neighborhood, the younger auditor turned to Harold Wong, and in a hushed voice said: "I don't get it. You had him dead to right. Why let him off so easily?"

Wong chuckled at this opportunity to explain the practical side of life to his assistant. "You know as well as I we didn't have enough evidence to guarantee a winning case in tax court. We should have won, to be sure, but you have to weigh the risk of losing, the precedent that might result, and the time and cost.

"The settlement's good enough," Wong continued. "I sincerely doubt we'll see Mr. Smith again. In any event, you're missing the best part of all. We now have all his records, and all those contractors and tradesmen he paid with cash. We can retire on the spin-off work from this case."

They walked on to their car, enjoying the success of the day, and looking forward to the considerable work ahead.

2.

The Joys of Over-Regulation

September, 1999

"Ruling a big country is like cooking a small fish."

— Lao Tsu

It was almost too good to be true. The call came from an anonymous tip (as they usually do) about a likely fraud by some pyramid scheme promoters calling themselves the Universal Freedom Network.

"Where do they think up these names?" thought Corporal Laroux as he reviewed the notes of his conversation. The informant had named names, addresses, contact numbers, and had even given the date and place of the next "ra ra" meeting where, with any luck, the kingpins would conveniently incriminate themselves.

A complete brochure was on its way in the mail; should be here the day after tomorrow.

The Home Team

The first thing Laroux did was to set up a meeting with John Blackmore of the secret service, since the operation was definitely active in many different countries. John in turn suggested bringing in Matt Mortimer from the federal consumer protection department because of his expertise on network marketing.

The more they talked about it, the more their task force grew: Peter Maverick of the securities commission; Jennifer Lightway from the attorney general's office; and Harold Wong from the tax department (just in case they couldn't make criminal charges stick, they might still get the money).

The day arrived for their meeting, and everyone came with their files containing the materials from the informant which had been duly distributed.

"Now that we're all here" said Corporal Laroux (lawyer Lightway had come in twenty minutes late), "and since you have all read the file" (there was a fluttering of paper as the rest opened their folders for the first time and began to scan the contents), "it looks like there's probably a fraud going on here in which a lot of people will lose a lot of money. My job is to investigate, but it's up to you people to prosecute the offenders."

"My first concern," interjected Blackmore, "is to ensure the confidentiality of this joint investigation. Do I have everyone's complete agreement that everything, and I mean *everything*, will be kept under raps, no leaks to the media, and so forth?"

Blackmore's roving eyes came to rest on Laroux, who shifted uneasily in his chair (the police were not considered particularly adept at keeping secrets from the press). The others casually nodded their agreement with suitably serious demeanors. Laroux followed suit.

"I guess the next issue," continued Ms. Lightway, "is who has jurisdiction, or primary jurisdiction in this case, since it's pretty clear this pyramid scheme as you call it, if that's what it is and we can prove it, is breaking a bundle of different laws. I haven't researched the area yet – I'll put some people on it – but there's the *Criminal Code*, the *Securities Act*, the *Pyramid Act* and the *Income Tax Act* for starters."

They continued talking among themselves, identifying suspects, correlating evidence, developing strategies – wiretaps, surveillance and the like. Everyone left the three-hour meeting in an upbeat mood.

They returned to their departments and duly filed their reports, which were distributed to their superiors and other interested departments for further filing.

The Defense Team

Meanwhile, on the other side of town, the would-be culprits had gotten wind of the investigation, and were huddled together with their lawyers in a rather large, dark-paneled boardroom.

There was significant money at stake, so the four promoters had retained the largest and best law firm in the city, only to be told they each had to have their own lawyer to avoid potential conflicts of interest. Although they figured this was to protect the lawyers from their regulators, they had no choice but to comply.

So there they were, four businessmen with their four high-priced lawyers from different firms, some with junior associates, seated in leather chairs around an exquisitely expensive mahogany boardroom table built in a previous century. They estimated the combined cost of their defense team exceeded $2,000 per hour, and they had already been there for over an hour!

Charlie Smith, the most talkative and self-appointed spokesman for the group, was the first to break.

"So what are you saying?" Charlie blurted. "I mean, according to you, they can both shut us down, and tie us up in lawsuits for years. They can each take a run at us, either one at a time or at the same time. There are so many laws they can use against us, we don't stand a chance if they decide to come after us!"

"You are essentially correct, Charlie" replied his lawyer, Walter Fulham QC. Charlie bristled from this familiarity from his lawyer, who was younger and also over-paid in his opinion. "But you have to appreciate the delicacy of your situation.

On the One Hand

"You and your associates have started this networking business that basically offers people access to offshore services, which they then sell to others for a commission," Fulham said. "Let me tell you exactly what the ever-vigilant guardians of our country are thinking," and he proceeded to summarize the myriad laws and regulations that could be used against his client.

"We have told you it is a matter of interpretation" (to Charlie, this was a lawyer's way of saying you could lose big time). "We are prepared to help you, but you must realize that this type of business is, to say the least, very aggressive, and bound to meet with stiff resistance from these government agencies," Fulham summed up. "And yes, they do have the power, working together, to make your lives miserable, and extremely costly, by starting numerous investigations, hearings and actions against you."

"This is intolerable," Charlie retorted. "With so many complicated laws, businessmen like us probably break one law or another daily and don't even know it. This country interferes with so many aspects of our lives that we have no privacy left."

Charlie basked in the attention he was getting, even if he was paying for it, and decided to wax eloquent as if he were addressing prospective recruits for his network.

"Allow me to illustrate my point," he continued. "Our government provides armed forces to protect us from violence; medicare to protect us from disease; welfare to protect us from poverty; pension plans to protect us from old age; consumer protection from crooks; environmental protection from pollution; and on and on.

"If it moves, it apparently needs protection, and is therefore subject to tax," Charlie said. "The more protection, the more tax; and the more tax, the bigger government gets. I ask you, where does it end?"

There wasn't a dry eye in the house. Charlie could see that from the sympathetic looks he was getting from everyone.

"Yes, well, we are not here to solve society's problems," began Walter Fulham dryly, when his junior spoke up.

Slight of Hand

"Have you thought about taking your network into cyberspace?" At twenty-nine, Jonathan Goodlad was one of the new breed of computer-savvy lawyers, and therefore something of a curiosity to his boss, who decided to let him have his say. Quite frankly, at this point he couldn't do any harm.

"It may be," Goodlad began a little nervously, "that the best way to protect yourselves is to move to a different jurisdiction. You could set up your computer server in an offshore financial center, where it would be beyond their reach. We have to remember their authority still stops at the border, and not every nation regulates its citizens to the extent we do, as Mr. Smith has emphasized.

"There are many offshore centers where the Universal Freedom Network could operate," he said, "unencumbered by the morass of regulations which have entangled it here."

Mixed metaphors aside, young Mr. Goodlad was making a lot of sense. Walter Fulham could see his associate had made a

favorable impression on the group that would result in significant fees for the assembled law firms. The promoters were already discussing ways of adapting the marketing plan.

Fulham chuckled to himself as he recalled the old saying "When a door closes, a window opens".

Regulatory Reactions

No one was more disappointed than Corporal Laroux as he finished dictating what would be the final memo to his file: "The suspects appear to have moved their operation offshore. We have therefore suspended the investigation unless substantive evidence of actual crimes being committed here becomes available."

The other civil servants prepared similar memos and closed their files, except for Harold Wong. The tax department frowned on walking away from an investigation empty-handed. He had to justify the time he had spent on the file, and ordered up the tax records for the last seven years on each of the promoters.

Who knows; maybe Wong would succeed where the others had failed.

3.

Raging Tax

November, 1999

"He who has his thumb on the purse has the power."
— Otto von Bismark

The choice was far from clear. Charlie Smith was reviewing his three handwritten pages on which he had meticulously listed the pros and cons of changing to another country. As his eyes flickered back and forth, his lawyer's latest advice reverberated at the back of his mind.

"Like it or not, taxes are the price we pay for living in a civilized society," Walter Fulham QC told him during their last meeting over lunch at his swanky private club. Ordinarily Charlie would not be caught dead in such a posh place, but there was a certain clandestine surge of importance that overcame him when he was catered to by the establishment.

So Charlie put up with the rich food, good drink, and his pontificating lawyer, who charged too much – even if he had kept Charlie out of the clink over the years.

Status Quo

"In this country we enjoy a high standard of living – medicare, education, transportation, communications, and so on," Fulham said. "Regrettably, these come at a cost, which is high taxes. With high taxation comes a huge government bureaucracy to administer it. In other words, legions of civil servants to collect the taxes, spend the taxes and, naturally, go after those who are not paying their fair share as they see it."

Having finished his third pint of lager by this point, Charlie's eyes started to glaze over; a fact not lost on his attentive lawyer who knew the seriousness of his client's predicament.

"Let me cut to the chase," Fulham continued, leveling his eyes with Charlie's. "The simple point is that everyone's financial situation here is literally an open book to nosy authorities, who have so many laws entitling them to snoop, their hardest decision is probably which one to use.

"The tax authorities can enter any place where a business is carried on, where property is kept or anything is done in connection with the business, or any books and records are kept or should be kept. The only good news is they have to get a warrant before they can enter your home, which is not hard to arrange.

"Once in, they can inspect, audit or examine your books and records, and any other property and inventory; and require you to render all reasonable assistance and answer all proper questions," Fulham said. "Since an investigation or audit is an ongoing process, they may come back as many times as necessary until the job is done.

"They can require you to provide any information and make copies (which is highly recommended since they don't have to return originals until the investigation has run its course). They may convene a private hearing.

"Finally, they have the power to seize and take away documents, and keep them indefinitely."

As Fulham stopped to catch his breath and reached for his wine glass, Charlie saw his chance and took it. "Then *qui custodiet ipsos custodes?*" he replied with a characteristic twinkle in his eyes. He may have quit school when all of twelve, but he had picked up a few things here and there during his fifty odd years.

"You never cease to impress me Charlie," Fulham said mid-sip. "Of course it is we, the people, who guard our guardians by casting our votes at each election."

"I suppose it beats some countries," Charlie added dryly, "where the tax police carry automatic rifles and shoot their way into your home if you don't let them in when they come to call. The rub is the people who really run this country are not elected and spend their entire careers interfering with our lives."

The Downside

Back at his home – built with lots of tax-free money – Charlie continued pondering his choices. Harold Wong, his nemesis at the tax department, showed no signs of going away. Charlie had tried everything, even visiting Wong in the filthiest, smelliest clothes he could muster and pleading poverty.

Wong simply had no heart. What he did have was the mandate of an ever-more intrusive government that was multiplying its confiscatory laws at an alarming rate in order to squeeze the maximum out of its citizens.

A lifetime of toil, scrimping and saving was threatened with annihilation. Of course, Charlie had cut a few corners here and there, to get to where he was. The trouble was, after the tax department added in its penalties and interest over all those years, there was quite literally nothing left.

Why had he put the house in his name? "You'd think you

would have learned after that blasted partner of yours decided to sue you a few years ago," Charlie thought, focusing back on the pages of pros and cons in front of him.

The Offshore Option

The thought of starting over was a disquieting one for Charlie. He was no spring chicken ready to go out and conquer the world. He liked his lifestyle, and didn't particularly want to move. At least he only had himself to convince, with his wife and children gone. (This was another financial setback that took years to rectify.)

"You could move to one of the offshore islands," he said to himself. "British tradition, strict confidentiality, no income taxes, and best of all lots of tourists looking for a better life for you to help, for a fee of course."

There were many island nations that ranked highly in his notes. For a modest annual charge, Charlie could get a self-employed consulting permit; for a few hundred thousand dollars, he could get a renewable homeowner's card; and for a few hundred thousand more a residency permit which he could flash whenever he returned home.

Home – that was the stumbling block; the place where his heart was. "A man's got to have ties," he thought, "but what do you do when the government squanders your money, and now uses half of it to pay interest to foreign money lenders?"

With a long sigh, Charlie flipped the pages, trying to come up with an angle where he could both have his cake and eat it too. Then he turned to a recent newspaper clipping which reported how the government was passing complex new laws to scare people from using trusts to shelter their money offshore.

"Bastards," he muttered as he read another about a report by the Committee for International Fiscal and Monetary Harmonization accusing countries with unfair tax competition.

"Since when did taxes become a competitive sport between nations?" he mused.

Going For It

Charlie Smith did not have sufficient wealth to relocate himself offshore, but he did have enough that he did not want to hand it over to the taxman. So he either had to lie down and take it, or move his affairs to a safer location. So he did.

The next morning Charlie visited his local bank and took out the largest permissible mortgage on his house in order to protect his equity.

Next, he contacted some offshore professionals recommended by his lawyer to set up a proper estate plan which conformed to the tax laws. What astonished Charlie was what could still be done despite all the government propaganda to the contrary. That gave him an especially warm feeling.

Within one week his offshore financial structure was in place, and the mortgage proceeds and his savings had been amalgamated at the bank. What followed was quite simple really. With the stroke of a pen, he signed the bank documents to wire transfer all his money to a new offshore bank account, safely out of Harold Wong's reach.

Wong's Tax Rage

Back at the tax department, Harold Wong eventually got wind of what Charlie did, but it was too late. There was virtually no equity left in his house. None of the other money Charlie had moved offshore attracted the much-vaunted departure tax on profits leaving the country. Charlie had simply left nothing within Wong's grasp.

Frustration did not begin to describe Harold Wong's state of mind. He determined the name and location of the offshore bank where Charlie had sent his wealth. Beyond that, he had no idea if the money was still there or had been moved elsewhere. The offshore bank safeguarded its customers' privacy, and its jurisdiction did not assist foreign tax investigations on the basis of long-established international convention.

Vowing revenge, Harold Wong locked away his files at 3:55 p.m. on that dismal day, and prepared to go home. As he put on his coat, he pondered the possibility of bringing back debtors' prison. Which was the furthest thing from Charlie Smith's mind.

4.

Baloney Banking and the Barracuda
January, 2000

"He that lies with dogs, riseth with fleas."
— George Herbert

The little box in the business section of the newspaper was more compelling by what it left to Charlie Smith's imagination, which could be very active indeed:

International Private Bank for sale.
Be your own banker and learn the
secrets of wealth creation known
only to a few.
Don't miss this opportunity.
Call today.

"That could be just the ticket for you, old son," he said to himself as he dialed the toll-free number.

Listening to a recorded message, Charlie might have known he was letting himself in for a lengthy and fruitless process. He had to reveal his name, address and telephone number in order to receive a description of the bank by fax.

Still, the recording was convincing, and promised the bank on offer was from a leading jurisdiction. Not knowing who or where they were, he put himself in their hands.

Days passed without any reply, so Charlie left a second message, suitably indignant to encourage the mysterious banker to respond. By this point curiosity had overtaken him, and he found his thoughts turning to the myriad ways he was going to use his new bank. Dreams of fantastic profits, status and respect kept him awake at night.

He simply had to have it.

The Plot Thickens

A single sheet of paper sitting on the fax machine announced the arrival of the bank. Actually, it was not one bank, but fourteen banks and eleven trust companies! They all had encouraging names like "Standard", "First" and "Global", and the banks were reasonably priced at $25,000 (the trust companies were a little less). The question Charlie might have asked was how can there be so many banks for sale at one time? Instead he called the number on the fax.

"Yes" was the terse salutation.

"Ah…, hello…," Charlie proceeded tentatively. "I'm calling about your advert. I've got your fax which seems to be in order, but it doesn't mention where the banks are incorporated. I don't think I'll be interested if they are from a tropical island or banana republic. I've done some research and…" Charlie was cut short by a casual snicker from the other end.

"They are not from any places like that. What I'll do is fax you all the details later today. I'm sure you'll be completely satisfied." With that the conversation ended, and Charlie leaned back in his chair, clasped his hands behind his neck, and resumed his reverie about being an international banker.

An hour later three more pages arrived by fax that described the formation, laws and politics of the Dominion of Euphoria. Interestingly the Dominion did not appear to have a physical location – no piece of *terra firma* to call its own – which caused the old alarm bells to ring. Charlie decided to call his lawyer, Walter Fulham QC, to see what he knew about it.

Too Good to be True

Fulham's guffaws of laughter did not exactly fill Charlie with confidence. "Are they still selling those banks?" he managed at length. "The skinny is Euphoria was started ten or so years ago by some con artist who simply decided to bypass all the troublesome little details.

"He found a prophet in the Old Testament to be the religious basis of his new country, wrote a series of laws along the lines of established international financial centers, and even set up a consular office in New York where you can get copies. The country is not recognized by the U.N., and has about as much legitimacy as the mythical places in *Gulliver's Travels*!"

Unperturbed by this advice, Charlie decided to take a different tack and telephoned his old compatriot Jack Farr. It did not take him long to tumble onto what Charlie wanted.

"I know exactly what you need, but you won't get it for $25,000," Jack advised. "Try more like $50,000, and you'll need another $2 Million in assets if you want anyone to take you seriously."

After a brief silence, Jack said in his usual matter of fact way: "You need to see the Barracuda." Charlie had long ago decided

sharp.

the bloke did not have a funny bone in his body. But he could be relied on for effective if not necessarily legal solutions. "He'll see you next week if you can make the trip South to his country."

From Frying Pan to Fire

Señor Pedro Ramirez Gonzalez, alias "the Barracuda", was intimidating in his cream-colored suit, wide-brimmed hat and dark aviator sunglasses that hid his eyes from view. It was also the combination of the large *Presidente* cigar and the gold tooth which flashed occasionally when he spoke through the strong smoke. He extended his hand which sported a large diamond ring, and got right down to business.

"Mr. Charlie, I understand you are looking to start or buy a bank in a flexible jurisdiction," Señor Ramirez said. "This is *no problema* really, provided you have the money, a bank manager with the proper credentials, a business plan, and all the directors can pass a police check.

"The time is about six months, and the price is sixty thousands of United States dollars, plus expenses, payable in advance," he added. "Naturally the time and cost depends on which country you choose, and the requirements change too."

"How much capital is required?" Charlie interjected.

"Well, that also depends on the country, and some places also require that the bank must have an operating presence there," Ramirez continued. "*Por ejemplo*, in some places it is not permitted that you run the bank by remote control, and you must have extensive funding and banking experience.

"Other financial centers only issue licenses to Class A banks," Ramirez said. "A handful of isolated island jurisdictions suffer from none of these impediments, and are very reasonably priced.

How do propose to use your *nuevo banco*?"

"I have associates who have access to prime bank instruments which they trade on a weekly basis at a discount, allowing them to offer very substantial returns to their investors," Charlie replied. "This is an exclusive opportunity which is not available to ordinary people. We are dealing with one of the top fifty banks in the world, and will have access to the kind of trading normally reserved for the big banks.

"As they have explained it," Charlie said, "since this is a new business for me, using the bank for this trading program makes it much easier to attract investors."

"I see," observed the Barracuda pensively through the cloud of smoke around his head. "In that case, *Señor*, I would definitely recommend one of the more flexible islands. You do appreciate what you have just described to me is a kind of Ponzi scheme, which will depend for its success on getting an ever-increasing number of investors into the program and using their new money to make the interest payments.

"It does not matter to me how your *grupo* will make its money, but I must warn you about this fact," Ramirez continued. "It is well-documented that these so-called bank instrument programs do not exist, except in the minds of their promoters."

This was definitely not what Charlie wanted to hear. To make matters worse, he was beginning to realize he had wasted his time and money in making the trip. Who was this guy Ponzi, and where did he live?

"How can this be, Señor Ramirez," he blurted in frustration. "I have seen advertisements by offshore banks offering returns of sometimes 200% per year for these types of investment."

"*Por favor* do not misunderstand me," Ramirez responded sympathetically. "I cannot prove what I have said. There is a full report by the International Chamber of Commerce in Europe that says what I have told you – that these investment programs simply do not exist. But not everyone has read it, and I believe there are many investors who are willing to risk their money, especially when offered these kinds of returns.

"I would also caution you to be extremely careful where you advertise your investment *mi amigo*," Ramirez continued, "since having the offshore bank may not protect you if you personally reside onshore.

"In fact, you may not even wish to be a director of this bank, assuming you can find some nominee directors who you can trust. For an additional fee, I can provide this service to you, of course."

Reality Check

The meeting with Ramirez lasted another forty minutes, and in spite of his reassurances to the contrary, Charlie just could not see how it would work. He had enough experience with pyramid schemes to know they don't last long before collapsing like a house of cards. One thing was clear: he and his associates must have a little chat!

Despondent, Charlie returned to his hotel, sat on the bed and looked out the window at the crystal blue sea. A gentle breeze was swaying the palm trees slowly back and forth. On any other occasion he would be delighted by the surroundings.

He decided the only solution to his dilemma was to retire to the poolside bar and order a substantial number of those tropical drinks with the little umbrellas in them. Then he would look for another angle.

5.

The Hazards of
Swimming with Barracudas

March, 2000

*"The king's might is greater than human,
and his arm is very long."*

— Herodotus

"So Señor Ramirez," asked Charlie Smith, "what do you think of my idea?"

They were standing in the den of the sumptuous colonial home of Pedro Ramirez Gonzalez, alias "the Barracuda", looking out over his vast estate.

Charlie was impressed by the evident wealth Ramirez had amassed from his offshore trust business. This kind of endeavor appealed to Charlie, and he was certain he could do the same, with the Barracuda's help.

"Mr. Charlie, your plan to provide offshore services to clients in your home country *esta bien*," Ramirez replied. "We work with many intermediaries such as yourself. The sharing of fees is *no problema*, and we have *mucha experiencia* in these matters. How many clients can we expect from you each month, and what will be their financial profile?"

sharp.

"There is a growing number of people where I live who are fed up with the high tax high spend policies of our government," Charlie answered at length.

"Everyday I meet prospects who are not concerned about the legalities of going offshore," he continued. "Capital gains tax has always been controversial, since it is seen as a tax on money which is already tax paid. They say, 'I already paid tax on my income, why should I pay it again when I use this money for investing?' But I do not need to tell you any of this, *Señor.*"

A Meeting of Minds

The Barracuda could smell substantial new business to pick up the slack from his other contacts who were becoming more nervous, it seemed, on a daily basis. Apparently they were not prepared to do what it took to make the big money.

"It is always useful for us to understand how much our *amigos* know," he purred like the fat cat he was. "You clearly have a great appreciation for this opportunity and what your clients need."

"To answer your questions," Charlie continued, "most of our clients would be looking to set up a personal plan using a trust, a company and a bank account to allow their capital to grow offshore without tax and protected from creditors. I would think 100 clients per year is attainable."

Charlie did not see the flicker of delight cross the Barracuda's eyes, hidden by his dark aviator sunglasses. It was not the basic fees from 100 clients a year that interested him. Experience had taught him that out of every 100 people, there would be some who would want his other, more "aggressive" services.

After all, he had not accumulated the wealth befitting a man of his large stature by simply selling trust and corporate services. His offshore Standard Trust Company, operating for fourteen years, was known in the right circles as being able to handle cash from any source without asking difficult questions.

Thin Edge of the Wedge

Charlie returned home as the new representative of Standard Trust, having settled on an agreeable commission arrangement, ready to go to work. Little did he know the dangers waiting for him down the road. The Barracuda for sometime had been on the most-wanted list of at least two onshore governments for money laundering, tax evasion and securities fraud.

To say Charlie was walking into a hornet's nest would be an understatement.

"Operation Fisher King" was already well underway, and his meeting with Ramirez had been recorded by the kind of high-tech equipment used by big governments with unlimited budgets. Charlie Smith was now part of a very serious international investigation – not exactly the kind of fame he aspired to since his modest start in East London fifty-four years earlier.

With Charlie's appearance on the scene, the task force decided to gather the additional evidence which would come from his group.

Eighteen months passed before the time to strike was at hand. By this point, Global Wealth Group, Charlie's offshore business, had 137 clients, most of whom fit the profile Charlie expected. What he did not know, because he did not deal with their day-to-day affairs but referred them to Standard Trust, was the extent of the services some of them enjoyed.

Charlie had never been one to judge his fellow man, so he was the ideal hand to feed the Barracuda.

Operation Fisher King

The task force met on a Monday to finalize its plan of action. Jennifer Lightway of the attorney general's office had been liaising with her counterpart in the offshore country where Standard Trust was licensed.

"We have not yet convinced the local government that cooperation is in its best interest," she said. "They are standing by international protocol, and require proof of our allegations before they will act under their new anti-money laundering and serious crimes legislation."

John Blackmore from the secret service smiled at this last point, since he also served on the committee whose aim was to cause every country in the world to sign serious crimes legislation. The offshore countries had been predictably reluctant at first, until they were informed that to do otherwise would be to risk a public relations nightmare when they were shown to be protecting criminals and their ill-gotten gains from justice.

The war against drugs had not been particularly effective in stopping the flow of drugs, but it was doing wonders to stamp out harmful tax competition. This little country would be no exception, given time.

Also seated around the table were Peter Maverick from the securities commission; his interest was in the insiders who were using offshore structures to make huge trading profits. There was Harold Wong of the tax department; he was after the tax evaders. Last there was Corporal Laroux who would lead the raid on Standard Trust's premises.

"Do we have a green light for the search and seizure?" Laroux asked.

"No, and not likely to get it," answered Lightway. "We will

have to go with Plan B, and use the element of surprise without official sanction."

The meeting moved on to sorting out all the details of the operation.

Two Lightening Raids

Laroux and his men arrived at the offices of Standard Trust just as it was opening, talked their way past the receptionist, and before anyone was the wiser, were casually putting files in boxes and downloading computer data.

The Barracuda was not in the office that day, could not be reached, and his manager was unsure what to do. By the time it occurred to him to call the trust company's lawyer for advice, the police had removed the files and were heading back to their hotel to examine their booty.

The raid on Charlie's office was conducted by search warrant, so he was powerless to stop it. As a result of foresight not normal for Charlie, he had no client information except for a handful of new files in progress. They took these anyway, and also tried to get Charlie to make a statement which he declined, having learned long ago that assisting an investigation of yourself only helps the coppers.

The Standard Trust lawyer wasted no time in getting a Court Order for the return of the files, which was successful to a point. While they had to return the boxes and computer disks, Laroux and his team had sent the encrypted data over the internet to their headquarters. With enough time, they would unlock all the secrets of the Barracuda's dirty business dealings.

Ramirez was relieved to hear his files were safe, until he had a disquieting call from the local Minister of Justice whom he had carefully cultivated over the years. The Minister had been telephoned by Jennifer Lightway who advised him they had the computer files, and were working with the encryption programmer to decrypt them, a process expected to take upwards of two years. To save the state this expense, she was prepared to bargain. The Barracuda had forty-eight hours to think it over.

A Tactful Retreat

Not wanting to be a prisoner in his own country, Ramirez took the deal. After all, he had enough money, and he could always start a new business. It was inevitable, he was told, that the encryption would be broken. True to his inner nature, he agreed to turn over the decryption program in exchange for his continuing cooperation and a lenient sentence, consisting of probation and a relatively modest fine. Many of his onshore clients would not fare so well.

As for Charlie, another important lesson had been learned. In future, he would have to be more discerning in his choice of partners. With nothing on him, and their hands full chasing down the Standard Trust clients, the authorities strongly warned him to find a different line of work. To which Charlie agreed, but then, he always did.

6.

Dead Cat Bounce

May, 2000

"No man is an island, entire unto itself."

— John Donne

"You are truly the sly fox *mon ami*," thought Jean-Pierre Renard to himself as he tallied the egregious profits from his latest stock scam. "The way you created the appearance of trading volume using forty offshore companies was pure genius. Who would guess the trades which took the stock from pennies to above $60 per share were all arranged by *moi*?"

A man of big appetites, Renard was celebrating his latest win with champagne and caviar. His glamorous lifestyle was the result of a privileged upbringing in his native France, which exposed him to the finer things of life — private schools, extensive travel, fine food and wines.

During his early years in European banking, he became acutely aware that the career chosen for him by his father would not maintain him in the lifestyle of his youth. Now in his mid-forties, he had spent the last ten years organizing and promoting fledgling public companies in North America.

In every case, once these stocks reached their intended dizzy heights they faltered for a short while, which was explained away

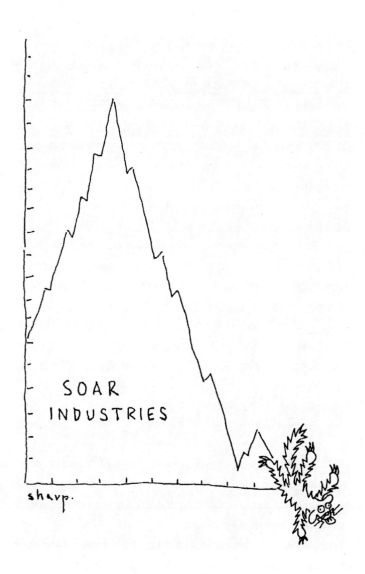

SOAR
INDUSTRIES

sharp.

as "creating a new base" to reassure worried investors. Then, they started their free-fall back to the pennies they started from.

Today's stock, "Soar Industries", had just finished its "dead cat bounce" after plunging from $63 per share, then recovering to $2.75 before settling in at yesterday's close of $0.06.

"Even the dead cat bounces when he is dropped from high enough," Jean-Pierre mused to himself.

In the beginning, due to his conservative training in the bank, Renard's name did not appear anywhere. Not as an officer, director, shareholder – nothing. There was no trace of him in any company records or the public files for securities regulators to use against him.

As time went by, his stock empire grew and the fox became bolder.

Eventually, Renard took greater positions in the stocks, sharing the take with fewer partners. This meant he had to disguise his shareholdings in order to avoid securities disclosure requirements and trading restrictions.

Offshore companies were ideal for his purpose. They came from around the world complete with nominee directors, but were still subject to his control. The perfect situation for his masterly stock manipulations.

Gone Fishing

While Renard was congratulating himself between sips of champagne, thousands of miles away securities investigators were meeting with regulators in one of the offshore countries which he used for his companies and trusts.

A team of four had been dispatched with a thick file compiled from years of rumors about his dirty stock dealings. The group was led by Peter Maverick, an investigator with the securities commission, his associate Liz Moranda, and two policemen specializing in financial crime, Corporals Laroux and MacReady.

The trip was the culmination of months of preparation and persuasion of the overseas authorities. The high costs of the investigation, compounded by the airfares, hotel and meals of this one-week expedition, made them keenly aware they had to crack the case here. All the more since this was the only jurisdiction that had agreed to see them, the others politely declining assistance to their "fishing expedition".

They met for breakfast in the pricey beachside hotel where they were staying. When they were seated with their selections from the fancy buffet, Peter Maverick opened the discussion.

"We must remember that we are here because the Minister of Finance agreed to see us," he said. "I don't know what to expect. A few years ago we wouldn't even get to first base in this country. We are about to put their new all crimes legislation to the acid test."

"In addition to this all crimes legislation," added Liz Moranda, drawing on her experience as a former securities lawyer, "I think we should stress the benefits of international cooperation between states and securities commissions".

The conversation continued about the best way to handle their upcoming meeting. Reviewing their allegations against Renard, they all knew the case was shaky. As they left for the meeting, nobody was giving odds on their chance of success.

A Meeting of Minds

The team was ushered into the boardroom at the Ministry of Finance and Corporate Affairs where they were seated opposite the

Finance Minister, the Deputy Minister for Corporate Affairs and three aides.

Maverick had barely started his opening remarks when the Minister raised his hand to interrupt. "Mr. Maverick, we know very well why you have come to our country."

Maverick's first thought was "There goes a $200,000 investigation". As his blood started to run cold, he vaguely heard the Minister say what he least expected to hear.

"We have reviewed the files at Provident Trust Company where Mr. Renard has his companies and trusts, including the trading records in the Soar Industries stock. We have them here for you.

"There is no doubt in our minds that, as a director of Soar, Mr. Renard acted in violation of securities laws," the Minister continued. "At the start, he held 32% of the stock through nine companies incorporated in this jurisdiction. They were all directed by him through the Renard Family Trust, which was administered by Provident. This evidence clearly shows he was in control and required to disclose his shareholdings."

The team returned home in triumph, laden down with enough files on Renard's trading activities to put him out of business for good.

As it turned out, the offshore island had opened its files more because of its fledgling stock exchange than its serious crimes legislation. It was just as concerned as the investigators to stamp out stock fraud by sharing information with other securities commissions.

"The world is truly shrinking," thought Peter Maverick as he readied himself to report to his superiors, and recommend the next step against Monsieur Renard. He was looking forward to teaching this rogue about the global reach of today's regulators.

Panic Sets In

Upon hearing of the investigation, Renard immediately contacted Charlie Smith, whose Global Wealth Group had set up most of his offshore companies.

"I thought you told me these companies and trusts were perfectly safe!" screamed an agitated Renard. "These tax havens were supposed to have secrecy laws which prohibit disclosing *mes affaires privées.*"

"With all due respect, Monsieur Renard, you never told us you were going to use the companies to violate securities laws," Charlie reminded him quietly. "I distinctly remember your saying that you were an active stock trader, not an insider of any company, and you needed so many offshore companies in order to segregate your various investments.

"The world is changing, and it's changing fast," Charlie continued. "Most offshore centers no longer shield serious crimes, and cooperate in big cases to protect themselves. You can't run anymore, at least not anywhere you'd want to live. I suggest you call my lawyer, Walter Fulham."

Resignation Takes Hold

Renard knew he was cornered with only one way out – a negotiated settlement. He had stashed away millions, so money was not an issue. The securities commission would probably agree to a minor fine and trading ban. After all, it was his first offence.

"I hate to disappoint you," stated Walter Fulham QC dryly, "but the awards in securities prosecutions have been steadily rising. Not knowing the full extent of what they have against you, you should expect a fine of perhaps $500,000 and ten years' suspension from trading public stocks in order to make this go away."

"Then why should I settle at all?" blurted Renard.

"Because, my friend, if you do not, the consequences could be very severe, including jail time," replied Fulham soberly.

Jail not being to Renard's taste, he settled for what turned out to be substantially more than his lawyer predicted – $1.5 Million and a twenty-five year ban from trading.

Perhaps retirement would not be so bad. After all, he was still free to spend his wealth on the finer things.

7.

How Martha Took It With Her

July, 2000

"We all live in a state of ambitious poverty."

— Decimus Junius Juvenal

The telegram from the Queen wishing her a happy 100th birthday arrived mid-morning. Martha Merryweather was thrilled. Born in the Commonwealth at the end of Queen Victoria's reign, she remembered fondly what it was like to be part of the British empire.

Her three children, eleven grandchildren, countless great-grand-children, and still more after them, would be arriving soon for the centennial celebration.

She still had a few hours left before the party in order to gather her thoughts for the announcement she had decided to make. Her decision to take matters into her own hands had resulted from the very unsatisfactory advice her long-time family lawyer had given her some months before.

Martha's Dilemma

"Martha," Henry Hollyrood had said somewhat condescendingly, "as your lawyer and close friend, I tell you there is no legal ability for you to do this. The taxman must have his due. When you pass on, your estate will have to pay heavy estate taxes. There will also be significant probate fees; and the legal fees will also be sizable due to your large family."

"Bullshit, Henry," she replied at once, not being one to mince words. "I am sick to death of hearing about what I have to do for the government.

"I have seen great changes in the world," she said, "and not all of them for the better. I remember a time when politicians worked for us, and government was limited to essential services. Don't you remember when we could lead our lives as we wished, free from interference, snooping, and these high taxes which are used for God knows what?"

"My dear Martha," Henry replied quietly. "May I suggest we are not here to debate society's ills, but to make some decisions about your estate so I can prepare your will."

"Don't you 'my dear' me," Martha retorted. He wasn't bad for a lawyer, but sometimes he forgot his place. "I haven't the slightest interest in helping the bureaucrats who have confiscated my life. I need more time to think about this," she concluded. "I'll call you with my decision."

A Different Approach

The doorbell snapped her out of her reverie. "That will be Charlie Smith," she said to herself as she heard the butler shuffling to the door.

Martha had been introduced to Charlie by a close friend who urged her to listen to him. He had apparently helped her friend, although she did not say exactly how. Martha had found him a little odd at first. The fact that he was short, balding and spoke with a common accent also didn't help. Still he had intrigued her enough to schedule this meeting.

"Good morning, Mrs. Merryweather," greeted Charlie as he entered the living room. "And may I say how radiant you look on this momentous occasion," he said with a flourish. Flourishes not being Charlie's long suit, Martha could not stop herself from letting out a little giggle.

"Thank you very much, Mr. Smith," she replied graciously. "Now let's get down to business, shall we? At my stage in life I don't have time for fluff. I need to make some decisions today, with your help," she said finally.

Martha proceeded to summarize her extensive financial holdings and equally extensive family.

"It has been said that the ideal estate plan is to spend all your money while living," Charlie said with a twinkle in his eye, "and then pay for your funeral with a cheque … that bounces.

"The more accepted approach, however, is to maximize wealth for the benefit of your family," he continued. "The big enemy of this is taxation, both during life and at death. At Global Wealth Group, we like to think of estate planning as applying specific tax avoidance strategies to preserve your family wealth so you can pass it on to your children and grandchildren."

"Let me put it this way," Martha interrupted. "My children are in their late seventies, my grandchildren in their mid-fifties, my great grandchildren their twenties and thirties. I have too many great-great-grandchildren to remember," she said. "The children and grandchildren are all very successful. None of my family needs any of my money, and I've always preferred them to make it on their own, which they've done."

"In that case, who is to benefit?" Charlie asked, bewildered.

"I think I should like to start a foundation to help

underprivileged children," Martha replied. "It must be tax efficient and kept out of reach of bureaucrats who might want to hijack its activities."

Problem Solved

"*No problema,* as they say in Panama," Charlie replied, "and that is just the place for your foundation. I would recommend a Panama Private Foundation as being suitable for your purpose. It is flexible, confidential, designed for charitable and family uses, and is both free from tax and regulatory interference. We have done this in the past, and our lawyers are most familiar with all the legal requirements.

"Panama is a civil law jurisdiction, and as such has had decades to observe the benefits and pitfalls of modern trusts as they have developed in rival common law countries," Charlie said. "Its solution is the private foundation, a hybrid entity that combines the strengths of companies with those of trusts. Like a company, the Panama Foundation is a juridical person, and its assets constitute a separate legal estate. Like a trust, it has beneficiaries instead of shareholders."

Due to the complexity of Martha's estate, Charlie decided to call his lawyer, Walter Fulham QC. "Charity is one of the few remaining areas that governments allow to function outside their tax regimes, for the moment," Fulham advised them over the speakerphone.

"There are various methods to avoid income taxes on Mrs. Merryweather's holdings when she transfers them to the new foundation," Fulham said. "Once there, they will be protected and available to carry out the foundation's charitable work."

They continued talking about the details until it was time for

Martha to get ready for her party. She invited Charlie to attend, which he readily accepted, looking forward to meeting further members of her well-heeled family.

The Announcement

Martha Merryweather was ushered to the podium in the grand ballroom with much fanfare. Looking out at the sea of faces of her family, she struggled to keep her composure as the applause died down. Charlie was seated inconspicuously at the back.

"My dears," she began, "thank you from the bottom of my heart. It is wonderful to be here with you today. You whom I have raised and taught; with whom I have shared good times and hard, and the life-giving experiences of family and community. You make me feel so proud.

"The best speeches are short, and this one will be no exception," Martha said. "As some of you know, I have been distracted lately by what to do about my estate. After consulting our family lawyer and others, I came to the conclusion there are others in the world who could benefit from it more than our government. It has not shown any great talent in how it redistributes our savings. I also reasoned that you would not receive any real benefit from it, since you do not truly need it.

"After much careful thought, and I trust with your support, I have decided to form *Los Niños Fundación* for the purpose of helping the disadvantaged children of this world. I have chosen not to call it the "Merryweather Foundation" because I believe family is a private matter.

"In order that its ongoing vision be assured," she continued, "there will always be three Merryweathers on the Foundation Council. I am confident that those of you who take on the duty

sharp.

will do so recognizing it is a public service, and outshine what today's governments have made tawdry.

"During the past 100 years, our family has prospered. This is not a bad thing – you will always come first in my heart. Now it is time that we turn our attention beyond ourselves and to the world outside, where through history, geography or plain bad luck children never get the chance to live and enjoy life as we do. Search your hearts, and you will see there is no other choice for all of us."

Martha returned to her seat at the table of honor, surrounded by the warmth of her family, and thinking about the extended family soon to come from around the globe. From his seat in the back, Charlie found himself fighting back an uncharacteristic tear.

He was a richer person for meeting Martha Merryweather.

8.

A Little Perspective
Leads to Big Problems

September, 2000

"Bad news travels fast and far."

— Plutarch

"You must remember that the Ministry of Finance is a law unto itself," said Charlie Smith to the reporter from Global Alarm magazine. "It has draconian powers of search and seizure, and if it wants you, it won't hesitate to contrive charges to arrest you."

"And this is what happened to you," prompted Max Fabler, an investigative reporter of eight years' experience. He already knew the answer to the question, but was interviewing Charlie to hear his side of the story. Not that his side would make any difference, of course. Fabler knew Charlie and his kind; they didn't deserve an even break. Besides, anything Charlie said would only detract from the article.

"Exactly," replied Charlie, seeing his opportunity to set the record straight. "It all started about two years ago, when I was approached by clients who wished to make sizeable investments in foreign jurisdictions. They were worried about the policies of their home government, and decided to diversify their holdings. This naturally included investing some of their funds outside their country." Charlie paused to make sure the reporter was taking it all in.

"What did they have to worry about?" asked a skeptical Fabler. "They're living in a wealthy democracy with one of the highest standards of living in the world."

"Well you might ask," continued Charlie, undeterred. "They did not seem to appreciate the amount of governmental intrusion at every level, the erosion of the rule of law, the suppression of the rights of individuals to those of the state. They saw rampant government wastage and pandering to special interest groups, and concluded they should protect their assets by placing some of them out of reach.

"Today these high tax, high spend governments are using the same scare tactics on the tax havens which have sheltered their wayward citizens," said Charlie. "Not content with bullying them at home, they are now exporting their tax imperialism to the rest of the world."

"Whatever," was all his eloquence earned from Fabler, unimpressed by this would-be Robin Hood. "Can we get back to the story? I believe you were at the point of moving your clients' investments offshore."

The Government Moves In

Charlie resumed his monologue, and as he talked, the chilling events came back to life as if they happened yesterday. There he was, in the small, drab room in the non-descript government building, being interrogated by a functionary from the enforcement branch of the finance ministry. They had moved swiftly, without warning, freezing all his client accounts and effectively closing down his business.

"Money laundering is a very serious crime, Mr. Smith, one that incurs stiff penalties," emphasized the gray man without emotion. "You would be well-advised to assist us in our investigation. These so-called clients of yours hardly deserve your protection. They are criminals, plain and simple."

Charlie's lawyer, Walter Fulham QC, spoke up at that point: "They may be criminals and they may not," he said, "that remains to be seen. From what we have heard today, you have certain suspicions without any evidence of wrongdoing. You have not identified these criminals.

"This is a fishing expedition," Fulham continued. "What you really want is for Mr. Smith to present his clients to you on a silver platter so you can review their cases and decide if, in fact, they have broken any laws. Therefore, my client must decline your invitation. Any legal process you care to commence may be served at my office. Good day to you."

With that, Charlie and his lawyer rose to leave, but were interrupted mid-movement.

"We anticipated that might be your client's response," said the investigator. "So we prepared this indictment which we are now forced to serve on Mr. Smith."

In one swift motion, the papers were served. Sheriffs entered the room, placed handcuffs onto Charlie's wrists and led him to the lock-up.

"Be seeing you," was the agent's parting shot. The government had won this round.

The Supertanker Approach

Charlie had never been in jail, and didn't like it much. However, principles are principles. He was not about to roll over

on his clients on account of some bureaucrat, even if he had to forego his liberty for a few hours.

Sitting there in a communal cell with common criminals, Charlie was hard-pressed not to succumb to his rising panic. What if he never got out? What if the really big guy across the cell with the tattoos took a special liking to him?

Charlie shrunk into his corner of the cell, desperately trying not to be noticed and praying for a speedy delivery from this purgatory.

Almost three days later, Fulham finally managed to get his client out on bail. A sober and shaken Charlie Smith was led from the cells and released to his lawyer.

"They've charged you with conspiracy to launder money," his lawyer said. "It is their way of telling you they are serious and coerce your cooperation."

"There are no grounds for these charges," Charlie replied. "You know that. Our clients are not guilty of these allegations. They organized their affairs to minimize their taxes. This is not tax evasion, and certainly not money laundering.

"Even if the government could make a charge of tax evasion stick," Charlie said, "how does that translate to money laundering? The latter crime requires criminal funds; the funds from our clients were clean and legitimate. If they later filed incorrect tax returns, how does that have any connection with me or with the funds themselves?"

"My friend," replied Fulham, "you are like a sailboat expecting a supertanker to change course because you have the right of way. These guys are big, powerful, and used to getting their own way. You, on the other hand, are small and in their way. You should be as nervous as a mouse in a pride of lions."

The case broke in Charlie's favor when a client came forward who was willing to go public and mount a legal challenge to the government's allegations. Not wanting to risk a public trial, the government finally capitulated on the courthouse steps, and released the frozen funds.

Charlie, however, was not so lucky. The trumped up charges against him remained. His best legal advice was to let sleeping dogs lie. Now he was having to defend himself again in the press, two years after the event.

Power of the Press

"Thank you for your time, Mr. Smith," Fabler said as he hastily made his exit. "What a load of nonsense," he said to himself back in his office as he began composing what promised to be a blockbuster article. He already had the inside version from the government who trusted him to have the good sense to tell the right story. He would not betray that trust.

The article required little editing after Charlie's interview, and was published the following week. The title – "Offshore Financier Wanted For Money Laundering" – said it all. It sketched the government's case with little detail, relying in great measure on the public's attitude that only guilty people get themselves arrested.

Fabler did mention he had contacted Charlie, but limited his remarks to criticizing his current activities. Not one to let the truth get in the way of a good story, he said nothing about the clients, their innocence, how Charlie stood up for them, or how the government eventually folded. The reader was left with the conclusion that Charlie Smith was the wrong company to keep.

Charlie's first reaction was to call Fabler and set him straight. After he finished ranting and raving to himself about yellow journalism, he reconsidered and called his lawyer.

"Let it go," was Walter Fulham's terse reply. "You won't

improve the story, and if you offend him he'll just write a follow-up article."

This was not what Charlie wanted to hear as he put the telephone down and poured himself a double Scotch on the rocks. A few minutes later the phone rang. It was one of his major clients who had read the article but knew the full story.

"To express our support and appreciation for what you did, I'm calling to let you know we are doubling our investment with your firm." This was the last thing Charlie expected to hear. As he prepared to go home, he kept thinking maybe there is no such thing as bad news after all.

9.

Watching Taxes Go Globallistic

November, 2000

*"The possession of power is inevitably fatal
to the free exercise of reason."*

— Immanuel Kant

Dumfounded was the word for it. For Charlie Smith to receive a call from the government was unsettling enough, but to be invited to attend one of its committees was incredible.

Alexa Powers, chair of the prominent Committee for International Fiscal and Monetary Harmonization, told Charlie his experience would provide invaluable insight. The next "plenary session" (governmentspeak for "big meeting" Charlie discovered from his pocket dictionary) was the following week, and his briefing materials would arrive tomorrow. With that, he was in.

Charlie's lawyer, Walter Fulham QC, could hardly contain himself over the irony of proposing Charlie to the committee. "What have you got to lose?" he asked. "At the very least you will gain a greater understanding of what the offshore countries are up against. Just think of the possibilities," Fulham chortled.

Charlie was reluctant at first – his being from the East end of London with a modest education. Not trained to mingle with the elite, he was a man of simple tastes. Still there was an irresistible urge to do it, and in the end curiosity got the better of him.

"How shall you profit from this opportunity old son," Charlie said to himself, sitting alone in his den as he swirled his scotch in its glass. Still dazed by the invitation, he was having difficulty focusing. "All in good time," he sighed as he turned out the light and locked the door.

The Big Countries' View

The committee meeting was well attended – more than ninety representatives from the large, wealthy countries were present, drawn entirely from their civil services. Alexa Powers took the podium for her opening remarks, and after the usual salutations got to the meat of it.

"As we all know, harmful tax competition threatens the stability of our global financial markets," she said. "Crises such as the Asian collapse wreak havoc and destruction which reverberate around the world. No one is spared the hardship that results.

"The purpose of this committee is to persuade, and if necessary, require renegade nations to harmonize their tax and banking systems with ours so that we are all on a level playing field," Powers continued. "Without a concerted and coordinated effort by our governments, the smaller, more mobile countries will continue to attract our capital.

"If we do not act decisively we may even be forced to compete with their harmful tax regimes in order to stop this drain. We cannot, and shall not, put our sovereign tax systems on the auction block for the lowest bidder," she ended fervently.

Looking around the room, Charlie noticed there was uniform approval of the chair's proposals. "What poppycock," Charlie muttered quietly, reminding himself he was only there to learn,

since clearly this group was too far gone.

"Allowing these high tax, high spend governments to harmonize taxes worldwide," he mused, "is like putting Dracula in charge of the blood bank."

The introductions concluded, the meeting broke into subcommittees, each assigned a group of offending countries to analyze and recommend remedies. Charlie found himself in a small group led by the strident Ms. Powers. Before he knew it, Charlie was the focus of attention, fielding all manner of questions about international financial centers and why people use them.

Powers was adamant that these wayward citizens and their tax dollars be repatriated to their home countries at any cost. Charlie could not help but have a grudging admiration for her dedication, even though the committee members seemed generally clueless about the real causes that fuelled the trend to international finance.

Smith's Perspective

When Charlie was asked for his comments on the committee's work, he suddenly felt himself looking into an abyss. "With all due respect," he stammered, "I do not have the benefit of the vast resources available to you." He paused to collect his thoughts.

"I might just observe that human nature – being what it is – people do not seem to like giving up the fruits of their labor where they don't believe they are getting value in return," he said.

"Good Lord," he thought, "did I actually say that?" Charlie quickly looked around the room, polling his unwanted audience for a reaction; there was none, only stony silence.

"I really have more questions than comments," Charlie continued. "Is this flight of capital caused by the tax havens or by the high tax, inefficient governments charging too much for the services they provide?" Again, there was no reaction.

"In accusing others of unfair tax competition are they really saying they want to hold onto their tax monopolies?" he asked. Still nothing; only blank stares.

"Are these governments promoting global financial transparency because they want to know everything about their citizens?" he asked in a louder voice, now in his stride. "Will there be any privacy or individuality left when they are finished?"

As expected, his comments fell on deaf ears. Still, Charlie welcomed the chance to observe first-hand this committee which was driving the international financial centers to distraction with their pronouncements, veiled threats and lobbying of the press.

Charlie left the meeting with two impressions: first, the Committee was blind in its defense of high taxes – no real surprise here; second, and more importantly, it was seriously underestimating both the offshore jurisdictions and its own citizens.

"Surely people want less government, not more," he thought as he got into his car to go home.

An Unexpected Visitor

The next day Charlie had an unscheduled meeting with Alexa Powers. She telephoned to say she would be at his office in ten minutes. She said she wanted to follow up with him on the points he made.

"Are the offshore structures that you form legal?" she asked.

"Naturally, provided you do not use them illegally," Charlie replied cautiously.

"Is your clients' money safe and protected from creditors?" she then asked.

"Yes, we only refer our clients to reputable firms who, I might add, expect us to refer reputable clients," he said.

"Do offshore banks protect their clients' confidentiality at all costs?" she continued.

"Short of protecting criminals, yes they do," Charlie said, growing increasingly nervous.

"Can your clients rely on your complete discretion in dealing with their affairs?" she asked.

"Completely," he replied again, "but I really can't provide you with any more information without jeopardizing our clients' trust."

"Excellent," she replied, "In that event, I would like to give you this," she said, handing Charlie a bank draft for $500,000.

"I don't understand," was the best Charlie could manage, wary that some kind of trap was about to be sprung.

"It's very simple," Powers stated emphatically. "The wealthy countries are intent on creating a cartel to coerce smaller countries to use a uniform tax system worldwide. They won't say it, but that is their agenda.

"Money laundering is being used as a back door to universal taxation," she added. "They want their taxes to remain high, and they want more people to pay them."

"Surely these governments will not be able to use money laundering forever to disguise their insatiable hunger for taxes," Charlie retorted, having relaxed a little.

Power's intense eyes bore into Charlie, making him wilt inside.

"It's clear there is a limited window of opportunity. The time to organize my affairs offshore is now. Can you help me?"

10.

It's a Small Bureaucratic World

January, 2001

"In the land of Listentoemholler
Steaks cost a nickel but the tax is a dollar.
How'd you like to live in Listentoemholler?"

— Shel Silverstein

Barreling down the street in his vintage Mercedes sedan, Charlie Smith slammed on the brakes and swerved to avoid hitting a boy on one of those shiny aluminum scooters.

"Why don't you watch where you're going!" Charlie shouted as the kid sped away.

"Why don't you slow down!" he yelled back, unphased by the close call.

A police officer who observed the narrow escape came up to Charlie. "May I see your driver's license, sir?" he asked from behind dark sunglasses that hid his eyes.

"Certainly officer," Charlie quickly replied, fumbling through his wallet. "Why does authority always rattle me?" he thought as he handed the license through the car window.

"Are you aware that this license has expired?" the policeman asked next.

"Oh brother," thought Charlie, "what more can go wrong?"

"Here is your ticket for exceeding the speed limit, and this is the ticket for driving without a valid driver's license," said the policeman. "You'll have to leave your car here until you renew your license, or get someone else to drive or tow it home."

Charlie detected the glimmer of satisfaction that small people with excessive power get when they ruin your day. "May I pull the car over to the curb and park it?" Charlie asked diffidently.

"Not without a license," came the cop's automatic reply.

"Then shall I leave it here, in the middle of the road?" Charlie retorted.

"That would be obstructing traffic," the officer replied. "I would have to give you another ticket, and have your car towed."

Charlie awoke with a start, his pajamas damp from the taxing dream. "Ask not what your government can do to you," he muttered as he checked the time. He was taking the Concorde to Europe for important meetings later that day.

"Better take a cab to the airport," Charlie thought; "no point in tempting fate."

Later, as the supersonic jet reached high altitude, Charlie looked down at the curvature of the earth. It reminded him of the astronauts' statements of how fragile and lonely it looks from outer space. He thought how small the world had become after all, with its rapidly disappearing diversity and trend towards conformity.

The Shrinking World of Banking

Charlie took a taxi from the airport to the Happy Taxpayer Pub for his first meeting with Jean-Philippe Couteau from the Banque Internationale. Halfway through his first pint of beer, he was not prepared for the bombshell his offshore banker was about to hand him.

"We must unfortunately decline to open any further accounts for your clients, Monsieur Smith," Couteau said. "And soon we will be reviewing all your accounts to determine if they may remain our customers."

"This is incredible Monsieur Couteau," replied Charlie quietly. "How long have we known each other now – two, three years? How can you just dismiss us with no notice or discussion? What has happened to the traditional loyalty between the private banker and his client?"

This conversation was making Couteau exceedingly uncomfortable. "Please understand that we have no choice in this affair," he continued. "The Committee for International Fiscal and Monetary Harmonization is gaining momentum with its policies. It has issued a warning against financial institutions dealing with corporate clients from tax havens.

"In addition, with the rapid computerization and expanding money laundering laws, soon all financial transactions will be tracked and regulated by *les grands gouvernements*," he finished.

"Monsieur Couteau," said Charlie, "you and I should be allies in this matter. We are the minutemen of international finance facing the tax imperialists. We've seen the whites of their eyes. Shall we defend the principles of individuality and privacy, or shall we run away?

"Bureaucrats want to know everything about us, so they can help us of course," Charlie continued tongue-in-cheek. "Our clients, and I sense a growing number of people everywhere are becoming very concerned about this intentional erosion of privacy being foisted on us by governments."

"Monsieur Smith, *je m'excuse*, but I have another meeting," said Couteau. "May I suggest we reconvene at my office tomorrow." As usual, Charlie paid the bill, and the two parted company.

Back in his hotel room, Charlie considered his options, and decided to call his lawyer.

Time to Regroup

"How could he just fire us like that?" asked Charlie in sheer frustration over the phone to Walter Fulham QC, his long-time legal advisor. There was a long pause before Fulham spoke.

"Well, he may have no choice," Fulham replied. "No banker likes to lose clients or money, especially if they can find another banker who will accept the business. That Committee for International Harmonization is driving everyone to distraction," he continued. "The banks and smaller countries are playing right into its hands, to the sheer delight of the bureaucrats who run it."

"We have never referred the bank a problem client," Charlie responded. "There has never even been a hint of money laundering, suspicious transactions or anything remotely illegal."

"Bankers today can't afford to offend the rich nations; eventually they get clobbered," replied Fulham. "My advice is you figure out what Couteau thinks he needs to continue the banking relationship, and see if there is any room for compromise."

Bankers, Umbrellas and Rain

"Monsieur Smith," said the banker at 10:00 a.m. the next morning in his spacious office replete with rich antiques and *objets d'art*. "Can we offer you *un café*?" Thus began the usual ritual of private bankers worldwide.

"And how can we assist you today?" Couteau said, as if nothing had happened the day before.

"After all these years," Charlie thought, "is this guy for real?"

He shifted uneasily in his Louis XIV chair as coffee was placed before him.

"As you know, an important part of our global business is to work closely with bankers," Charlie began. "We have an ongoing role between our clients and their bankers, their accounts and their investments."

Charlie fixed his eyes on the banker's: "Let me ask you, Monsieur Couteau: what type of banking business do you want?"

"I wish I could be more helpful," Couteau replied, "but this is internal bank policy which *je regret* I am not at liberty to disclose." Charlie did not believe what he was hearing.

"Then how must we structure our clients' affairs so that you will continue to accept them?" Charlie asked next.

"*Je suis désolé*, truly, Monsieur Smith," said the banker with his usual élan. "But I cannot reveal matters of bank policy. I am sure you will understand."

"What I understand, sir, is that your bank has chosen in effect to become an extension of the big country regulators." Charlie was furious and doing his utmost to maintain his composure looking across the desk at this pedant.

"No, let me put it this way: you have become a weapon of oppression in the hands of the globocops," Charlie hissed. "Good day, sir." Charlie abruptly rose and headed for the door, before he lost all control. He did not hear the banker's woeful entreaties to come back.

"Short arms, deep pockets," Charlie whispered as he entered the street and headed for his next meeting with the people he was certain would be his new bankers.

11.

Free Spirits and Drunken Bureaucrats

March, 2001

"If this is the best of all possible worlds,
what then are the others?"

– Voltaire

"Since the dawn of government, was there ever a time when bureaucrats didn't scheme and plot to control people for their own aims?" thought Charlie Smith, sitting in his office at Global Wealth Group.

"Robespierre's civil servants relieved 40,000 citizens of their heads before he lost his own to them during the French revolution, all for the purpose of redistributing wealth. Of course, times were harsher then and their methods cruder than today's governments.

"And what of Cromwell, the soldier turned dictator in seventeenth century England whose government created the Northern Ireland problem we have today?

"Mussolini made the trains run on time for the first time in Italy's history, but look what happened when he became the big cheese with no one to supervise him. Same thing with Hitler, Uncle Joe and Mao: how many civilians died under their regimes? Wasn't it 30 million?

"At least the bureaucrats now use taxes and regulation instead of death to wield their power against us," concluded Charlie before he was abruptly returned to reality by his receptionist announcing the arrival of his next appointment.

One of Charlie's clients had referred this new visitor with what he called "a tricky financial problem". Charlie liked new challenges, particularly when there was a fee in it for his company.

As Charlie ushered his new prospect into his office, he studied his face closely while he covertly scanned him for listening devices with a tiny hand-held monitor. Satisfied that he was clean, Charlie relaxed a little.

Baiting the Hook

Shawn Dupery was an unexceptional, middle-aged man, dressed in a drab suit and cheap shoes. But his eyes told Charlie there was far more than his outer appearance suggested. Both intriguing and disturbing.

"Mr. Dupery, may I say what a pleasure it is to have the opportunity to assist you," Charlie began with his customary flourish. "While I cannot comment on our mutual friend's affairs, let me assure you that his introduction will ensure you of our full and professional attention."

With that the two men sat down across Charlie's antique partners desk to exchange the usual pleasantries that disguise the sizing up process of business.

"Charlie, may I call you Charlie?" Dupery started tentatively. He received a nod in reply. "Good. My circumstances are probably not that unusual to a person of your experience. I have a little problem that I hope you can help me with. Over the past several years I have accumulated $9 Million in cash which I'd like to invest."

"Where, might I ask, did these funds come from?" Charlie asked as delicately as possible, still examining Dupery's eyes for some hint to his character.

"I used to be in the gaming business in various parts of the world," Dupery said. "I worked for a large syndicate which, as you might guess, didn't like to pay taxes. Didn't care much for authority of any kind actually. As a consequence, my cash went straight from the slots and tables to the counting room and into my pocket."

Charlie paused to collect his thoughts. "In other words," Charlie told Dupery, "taxes have never been paid on these funds, which are still owed to various countries around the world." What Charlie didn't say was: "And they are the illegal skim from casinos that attract many criminal penalties".

Letting out Line

"You have it exactly," Dupery replied. "What I would like to do is have you set up a financial structure and invest my money in securities, mutual funds, real estate and so forth. I haven't given the mix of assets much thought, and would look to you for advice. For this service I am willing to pay you $500,000. In fact, I have it with me."

With that said, Dupery placed his attaché case on the desk, opened it and swiveled it to face Charlie. Before him were rows of neatly bundled $100 bills that filled the briefcase nicely. Big temptation, big risk.

"You are very persuasive, Mr. Dupery," Charlie responded, his eyes fixed on the cash. The left side of his brain was already creating ways to spend it, but the right side was in turmoil.

"Regrettably," said Charlie, "I cannot take your money, what

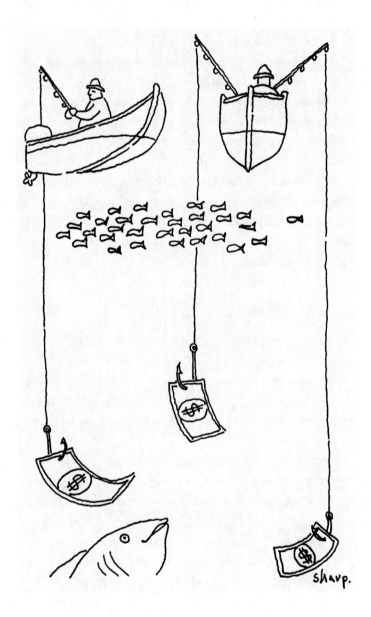

with the new money laundering laws. They are so wide-ranging in their definitions and their penalties that to help you could be my legal suicide. And with the new reporting requirements for financial institutions, it is very difficult to hide."

"Are you saying it is impossible?" Dupery asked.

"Not impossible," Charlie said turning his eyes back to the money, "just very difficult." There was a twinkling in each man's eyes that spoke volumes about a camaraderie often shared by men of the world.

"Shall we then say a fee of $1 Million?" added Dupery as he played with his coffee cup. Charlie was tempted to accept the challenge, but a sixth sense told him to wait a day and think it over.

"Mr. Dupery, you have got my full attention," Charlie said. "In complicated matters like these, we prefer to take a day or two to consider the ramifications and formulate a strategy." Dupery departed with his briefcase in hand.

Hook, Line and Sinker

Charlie shut the door to his office, and telephoned his lawyer, Walter Fulham QC. "What can I do?" Charlie asked. "A million dollar fee doesn't walk through the door every day. Surely there must be a way around this thing."

Fulham took his time replying. "I know you don't like lawyers who tell you that you can't do things," he replied, "but you can't do this. The money laundering laws are far-reaching. I know they are poorly thought out and politically motivated, but they are *very* broadly drafted, to your peril if you cross them.

"How could you possibly insulate yourself from prosecution?" Fulham continued. "You can hardly contact each interested government and settle on the taxes owed by this man, even assuming you could reliably figure out who's owed what, let alone the criminal sanctions involved.

"Furthermore, consider the long-term effects on the Global Wealth Group of being caught in a high profile money laundering case," Fulham concluded.

"So what can I do?" Charlie asked again, despondent.

"Given your position as a financial consultant, you have no choice," Fulham replied. "With the knowledge you now have, you run the risk of being charged as a conspirator when Mr. Dupery gets caught; and get caught he will, mark my words. I'm sorry to have to say this, but you must instruct me to contact the Attorney General's office and make a report to protect you and your business."

"It's against all my principles," Charlie replied reluctantly. "If you say I have no choice, then carry on."

One that Got Away

Charlie heard nothing for ten days, during which time he kept stalling Dupery with one excuse or another. Fulham finally called to say: "I've just received word from the AG's office that they are not going to do anything on this matter."

"What?" Charlie blurted, his mind racing.

"Apparently your Mr. Dupery is one of their undercover agents," Fulham continued calmly, "and they can hardly charge their own man."

In a way, Charlie was hardly surprised, but he was very uncomfortable that the government would stoop so low to fabricate this elaborate fishing expedition, all for the purpose of entrapping him. He had heard stories that there were more and more sting operations being used as the weapon of choice against crime, but this was the first time he had experienced it first hand.

As the initial shock of the news wore off, an overwhelming sense of relief came over Charlie. He had not been charged with anything. He was still free to do his business. Best of all, he had beaten the government at its own game.

"Will bureaucrats stop at nothing to achieve their ends?" Charlie thought. "They would entrap their own mothers, if they thought they could make an example of them. What a world – no privacy, intrusive governments, convoluted laws, rapacious bureaucrats..."

As usual, he was interrupted by the arrival of his next appointment.

12.

A Common Kickback Sting

May, 2001

"The best armour is to keep out of gunshot."
— Francis Bacon

Frankie "Four Fingers" Fabia was one happy camper. A small time crook with a record as long as his arm, he earned his nickname from ratting on his comrades to save his own skin. He'd paid the price for his indiscretion with his fifth finger.

Not one to grasp lessons quickly, now he was working for the police a third time as an undercover agent. It was almost becoming a regular job.

He was perfectly suited for the part, they said, since he knew his way around. Not only would they turn a blind eye to his many nefarious activities, they would even pay him 10% of any criminal proceeds they recovered.

There was another reason the police wanted Frankie for this particular job. A few months ago they had him cold. He was looking at seven to ten years for a minor extortion that had backfired, until they offered him the standard deal. If he gave them a bigger fish, he could swim away without jail time.

So, using the name "Shawn Dupery", he tried unsuccessfully to trap Charlie Smith of the Global Wealth Group into laundering $9

Million. But Charlie was too smart for him, and had his lawyer, Walter Fulham QC, report Dupery to the Attorney General. This forced the AG to admit Dupery was an agent, much to his chagrin. Not a man who liked to be embarrassed, the AG had now ordered a sting operation against Fulham. The police couldn't think of a better guy for the job than Frankie.

For his part, Frankie couldn't think of a better way to go straight, more or less.

The Mark

It was 8:00 a.m. Tuesday morning. Frankie was sitting in Fulham's favorite café sipping black coffee as he observed his quarry. Fulham was at the next table, digesting an article in the morning newspaper entitled "Committee for International Fiscal and Monetary Harmonization drops fight against unfair tax competition".

"And about time too," Fulham thought as he folded the paper and left for his office. Frankie followed at a discreet distance.

Fulham was just entering the elevator when Frankie came through the swinging glass doors of Fulham's building. Frankie immediately noticed the security cameras in the lobby, and used his newspaper to shield his face from view.

"Is there no privacy left?" he asked himself as he counted to twenty before going up to Fulham's office.

"Would it be possible to see Mr. Fulham?" Frankie politely asked the receptionist. "I don't have an appointment. Please tell him it's about new business."

"Certainly sir," she replied, "and may I have your name?"

"Frank Subrosa," Four Fingers said, not missing a beat. "I wonder what bugging devices they have in here," Frankie thought

as he waited for his host to appear. Of course, he was wired to the hilt by his employers.

A few minutes later Fulham emerged from his office and extended his hand in greeting to Mr. Subrosa. The two men moved to a mahogany-paneled conference room replete with antique furniture where they could talk undisturbed.

Frankie was impressed by the style of this place. Another time, another place, he could maybe even get to like this guy.

The Sting

"Now sir, how can we help you?" Fulham said from across the Louis XIV table.

"Mr. Fulham, or may I call you Walter?" Frankie asked to an affirmative response. "Fine, Walter it is," he said. "I am told you are an international lawyer who knows how to get things done.

"You see," Frankie continued, "I have quite a lot of money that I have earned, but not declared for tax purposes. Now I want to bring that money back into the system."

"Two questions," said Fulham. "How much money are we talking about, and what form is it in. Is it cash or is it in a bank?"

"Not much; about $2 Million. And yes, it is in a bank, under an assumed name," Subrosa replied. "What would be your fee for handling this transaction?"

"Our standard fee is 10%, so $200,000," said Fulham, wary of this new client but always willing to take on new business.

"That is acceptable," came the welcome reply as Subrosa eased back into the comfortable chair.

The two continued to discuss wiring details, signed a standard retainer agreement, and agreed the transaction would occur next Friday, which it did.

"Mr. Fulham, I am Corporal Laroux and this is Corporal MacReady. You are under arrest for money laundering."

Despite his many years' experience as a lawyer, Fulham felt his resolve crumble and his knees go weak. He sat down, his mind racing.

"I beg your pardon," was the best Fulham could manage in reply, looking up at the two imposing policemen.

"You'll have to come with us to headquarters where you will be formally charged, fingerprinted and bail arranged," continued Laroux routinely. "Due to your reputation we will dispense with the handcuffs."

The two officers led Fulham past his shocked staff to the awaiting police car and jail.

It took four hours to go through the formalities before Fulham was released. His next step was to retain his long-time colleague and friend, Marvin Lexter, one of the leading criminal defense lawyers.

Lexter's expertise was fighting constitutional cases, which he likened to "defending David against bureaucratic Goliaths". He had amassed an impressive list of wins over the years, and the mere mention of his name sent fur flying.

You never really know what it's like until it actually happens," Fulham told his lawyer. "After all these years, to be treated this way, to be embarrassed in my own office, to be..." He was cut short by his lawyer.

"Walter, forget it," Lexter replied abruptly. "This is a serious matter. You have attracted the government's attention, which will use due process of law to its fullest extent.

"If, and I say *if*, we get you out of this mess," Lexter

continued, "it will take at least six to eight months, maybe longer. During that time you will not be allowed to leave the country. You have been accused of a criminal offence, and are being watched closely. Just make sure you are a model citizen until we sort this out."

The Defense

The two jurists spent what felt like years to Walter preparing for trial, constantly hampered by the AG's ongoing refusal to supply information. It took Lexter no fewer than eleven pre-trial motions to compile the evidence he needed to prepare his client's defense.

As Lexter reviewed the AG's evidence, that defense became clear. It would be a jury trial.

Fulham was lucky. Perhaps due to his standing in the community, the vagaries of a jury trial, or maybe the rising intolerance of government interference in our lives, he was found not guilty on all counts. Taking his lead from the jury, the judge used the opportunity to slam the AG and his propensity to entrap citizens into crime.

"This Court finds it particularly disturbing that the Attorney General, who represents the government, and whose role is to promote the rule of law, should actively engage in entrapping its citizens," said the judge reading from his notes.

"There was no crime here. An agent of the government intentionally fabricated a falsehood that would never result in criminal activity but for his efforts.

"This court cannot and will not condone such conduct by our government, designed to entice otherwise honest people into committing crimes as defined by that very same government," continued the judge. "My only hope is this court can, by this decision, send a clear message to the government that it is there to serve the people. Not to entrap them into crimes that they would otherwise not commit.

"As is my discretion in these matters," the judge concluded, "I further award full costs to the defendant."

This was welcome news to Fulham, who had so far spent $300,000 on his defense.

The Take

A few days later, Frankie was summoned to the station for a meeting with Laroux. "Well, Frankie" Laroux said, "all I can say is it didn't go well. Fulham got off and the AG is as mad as a hornet.

"The good news is your other operation netted $29 Million for the government, earning you a cool $2.9 Million. Don't spend it all in one place."

As Frankie looked at the official cheque for $2.9 Million, his foremost thought was how he could get the money offshore out of the government's reach. His next call was to Charlie Smith, who Frankie felt certain would know how to handle his hard-earned take.

From Frankie's point of view, he was just evening up the score.

13.

Postcard from Paradise

July, 2001

*"The thirst after happiness is never extinguished
in the heart of man."*

— Jean Jacques Rousseau

Looking into the barrel of a twenty gauge shotgun is disconcerting at the best of times. But to be awakened in bed by a thief standing above you is terrifying. So thought Charlie Smith as he slowly got out of bed, hands in the air.

Charlie was keenly aware he was in a Third World country with no one to help him. Especially since the gun had been taken from the sleeping security guard outside.

"Give me all your money," came the nervous demand from the lone gunman. Resisting the temptation to act out his James Bond fantasy, Charlie handed over the contents of his wallet. The way he figured it, his life was worth more than $327.

What happened to Charlie that night was a graphic illustration of the trouble you can find in so-called Paradise. People living in rich countries can take a lot for granted that goes out the window when they move to poorer places. Charlie had learned during his short time in international finance to do his research and never assume anything.

Take buying property in a foreign country, for example. People typically go to holiday spots on packaged vacations where they are overwhelmed by time-share salespeople. These days they tend to sell interval ownership, where all you buy is the owner's promise to let you stay at his property for one week a year. What the high-pressure sales pitch tends to omit is how the promise can be abruptly cancelled by the owner's bankruptcy, acts of God and so forth.

It's a business that appealed to Charlie's sense of larceny when he figured out the time-shares sold for 300% of the property's market value.

People who decide instead to purchase property outright quickly learn they must basically create an island within an island. Otherwise they place themselves at the mercy of the shortcomings of their adopted country. A generator to supplement unreliable electricity. Satellite communication for dodgy telephone service. Reliable tradesmen to fix things properly. Security guards (preferably ones that stay awake) for that extra sense of protection.

Perhaps even the son of a Colonel to insure the success of a new business.

Charlie the Beachcomber

Sitting by the beach, sipping his gin and tonic, Charlie was pondering the endless challenges that accompany the opportunities of doing business overseas. Getting replacement parts, not being cheated by local merchants, communicating in different languages.

"What I need is a voice-activated universal translator," thought Charlie as he watched the activities on the beach. "Most of those people will go home in a week with memories of an idyllic place that offers all the things they lack at home. Mostly freedom from constant governmental interference in their lives," he continued to himself.

"I may not be the brightest crayon in the box," Charlie said aloud as he rose to leave the beachside bar, "but there must be something I can sell those people besides tee-shirts and postcards."

Charlie was in a quandary. He was not happy unless he was busy selling something to, or taking something from, somebody. And there certainly were a lot of bodies on that beach behind him.

Charlie decided later his best idea ever hit him as he reached the dusty road full of street vendors and distressed cars. He simply had to find a way to sell his offshore financial services during his stay on this island. What better way than on the beach, where there was no rent to pay?

Global Webspinner

The next day Charlie put his plan into action. He started by having a small sign made with the words:

Global Wealth Group
Offshore Financial Services
Private Consultations
Confidential Advice
Enquire Here

It only took him one week and two false starts to organize the sign – good printers were in short supply.

Lounging on the beach in casual clothes and dark glasses under a sun umbrella, beer bottle on the side table, Charlie was reading one of the latest offshore magazines. Others were piled beside him, along with various books on the subject. His sign was

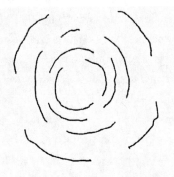

GLOBAL WEALTH
GROUP
OFFSHORE

PRIVACY
RUN AWAY
FREEDOM
GOING OFF

sharp.

firmly stuck in the sand. You wouldn't know it to look at him, but Charlie was ready to pounce on the first unsuspecting tourist to stray into his web.

It only took twenty minutes before he heard a voice beside him say: "Excuse me, do you have a few minutes to discuss my situation?"

Charlie looked up and saw an attractive fortyish woman in a bikini, loud shirt and straw hat. "Perfect," thought Charlie as he invited her to sit on the lounge chair beside him.

"What exactly do you do, Mr. Smith?" asked the prospect between sips of her rum punch.

"I like to think of myself as a designer," answered Charlie.

"Really; and what do you design?" continued the woman, noticeably confused.

"Escape routes," said Charlie with a characteristic twinkle in his eye. Seeing the bewilderment on the woman's face, Charlie continued. "We are all looking to escape some form of threat in our lives. Maybe it's a creditor, a soon-to-be ex-spouse, or the taxman. Through our skillful handling of international banking, we restore the freedom that our clients miss in their home countries."

"I see," the woman replied thoughtfully. "In my country, the laws are so complex now that I worry whether international financial structures are still legal."

"In the immortal words of Jonathan Swift," Charlie replied effusively, " 'Laws are like cobwebs, which may catch small flies, but let wasps and hornets break through.' Are you a fly or a hornet, Miss …?"

"Victoria Cheethem," the woman replied. "Let's say I prefer to be a hornet, but have never tested the web." Now there was a twinkle in her eye that more than matched Charlie's.

"My husband and I recently divorced, and my settlement

amounted to about $6 Million, plus some properties," Victoria said. "I don't have much experience in these matters, and would like to invest most of that money offshore. After years of supporting my husband, it's time I took control of my life."

Victoria and Charlie talked about the intricacies of global wealth management for hours, adjourning first to the bar, then dinner, dancing and finally her hotel room. Charlie was impressed with how fast she grasped complicated financial concepts. The more he told her, the more she wanted to learn. She was very enthusiastic.

The next morning over breakfast Victoria informed Charlie she had been unexpectedly called home, but would return in a week to continue planning her affairs with him. Charlie assured her he would be there for her as he kissed her good-bye at the airport security checkpoint.

Victoria's Secret

After weeks passed and the romance of his encounter faded, Charlie called his lawyer, Walter Fulham QC, for a background check on Ms. Cheethem. To say Charlie was disappointed by the report is not to know him; intrigued better describes his reaction.

"Victoria Cheethem," said Fulham, "is wanted by police agencies in at least four countries, not to mention some very bad people. It is alleged her money is the proceeds of crime, from her activities as a high class madam to assorted crime bosses."

"In short, she's on the lam," Fulham concluded. "With the new money laundering laws, the fortune she amassed is subject to seizure. Unless she has some very good professional help, I wouldn't rate her chances of keeping that money as very high."

Months passed without a word. Then one day Charlie received

a postcard at his office, having returned from Paradise to enjoy the refinements of life not found there. It read:

Dear Charlie,
Thank you so much for your advice which enabled me to protect my assets from certain unworthy creditors.
Life is not fair, but you helped me when I needed it most. I hope our paths will cross again soon.

Yours, Vicky

"In other words," a sober Charlie reflected, "she took my best work and used it to save herself. Here's to you, clever Victoria," he said, raising his glass to have his first drink of the day.

He knew he had been suckered by the oldest game in the book. Who knows; someday they might meet again so he could return the favor.

14.

Privacy Lost and Found

September, 2001

"The people's good is the highest law."

— Cicero

Jimmy the Juice was a little uncomfortable as he walked past the booths at the Worldwide Web Porn Convention. It was not the subject matter that bothered him; pornography had been a mainstay of his diverse criminal career. The fact was the internet had passed him by, leaving him perplexed by the tantalizing amount of business just beyond his grasp.

Jimmy was a stocky man in his late fifties who had grown up on the street, the hard way. He'd served time for various misdemeanors as a kid, but not for his serious enterprises. He was nobody's patsy, and prided himself in his twelve-year record of eluding the law.

A Virtual Casino

"Excuse me, sir," asked a voice from a booth. Jimmy turned to see a short, balding man with glasses in a drab suit. He was standing under a banner that read "Global Wealth Group Encryption Solutions".

"Would you like to hear about our 1,024 bit encryption program that ensures your privacy on the web?" asked Charlie Smith.

"Not really," replied Jimmy, ready to punch his lights out if he came any closer. Not to mention he didn't have a clue what the guy was talking about.

"Perhaps you might be interested in our online gaming package that allows you to have a virtual casino not regulated by the authorities?" continued Charlie. "Or maybe one of our adult site software programs…" Jimmy wasn't listening as he considered the possibilities of an unregulated casino.

"What do you mean by *unregulated?*" Jimmy asked while Charlie was still talking.

"I have a brochure describing the package in detail," replied Charlie. "Why don't you sit here so I can briefly tell you about it?"

Reluctantly, Jimmy entered the booth and sat down at a small table with two chairs. "As you can see from this diagram," said Charlie, "the online gaming package has four components: a computer server that is placed in a secure country; an offshore legal structure that avoids regulatory and tax problems; banking facilities to handle payments; and our exclusive, encrypted gaming software which, I might add, is one of the best in the business."

"What is a server?" asked Jimmy, again interrupting Charlie mid-sales pitch.

"Who is this guy?" thought Charlie as he continued what would be a fifteen minute introduction to the internet world. When Jimmy left, he understood little more about the internet, but he did know one thing: he could hire a computer expert to run it. As long as the person was loyal to Jimmy.

A few telephone calls later, one of Jimmy's longtime associates suggested his nephew for the job. The boy was a real genius when it came to computers, his associate said, so Jimmy agreed to meet him.

The next day, Jimmy found himself talking business with a twenty something geek wearing glasses, a white tee shirt and jeans. "What am I getting myself into?" Jimmy asked himself as the kid gave him a far too complicated explanation of his abilities, internet gaming and something called "the web".

No doubt about it, the kid was enthusiastic, and seemed to know his stuff. "But how can I get him to stop talking?" thought Jimmy as the other prattled on.

Jimmy put the nephew together with Charlie, and within a few months had a thriving internet gaming business. He was even getting advertising revenues from something called "banner ads". Maybe there was something to this new electronic business. The way he understood it, he could do this business anywhere in the world with complete anonymity. He liked that a lot.

Unwanted Attention

Over at the Center for Internet Studies, a clandestine arm of the secret service, John Blackmore was reviewing files when one of the computer specialists came in. "We're picking up traffic from a new internet gaming site with unusually large transactions," he said, holding out a file.

"Explain," replied Blackmore as he took the file and started scanning it.

"We've been testing a new software system named Raptor that scans all internet traffic which contain key words or large sums of money," the specialist continued. "Key words include drugs, cash, offshore, tax haven, and the like. It can also intercept emails and crack encryption programs.

"A site calling itself True Blue Gaming has a high incidence of large bets and settlements. We think this could be a front for laundering illicit money," concluded the technician.

"What do you recommend?" asked Blackmore disinterestedly.

"We place a few bets, and use Raptor to trace the transactions into the True Blue server. We can then either extract more data or send in a team to seize the server," replied the specialist.

"Alright, do it," instructed Blackmore, "but keep me updated on a regular basis. I don't want this to bounce back at us, or expose Raptor to unwanted scrutiny."

During the next few weeks, the Center's super computers zeroed in on True Blue's server. They didn't stand a chance. The reality was, given enough time and money, the Center could crack anything. Since money was no object, coming in endless supply from complex government budgets that taxpayers could not fathom, that left only time on True Blue's side.

The Penny Drops

When Charlie Smith got the call from his panicked techie that the True Blue server security protocols had been breached, he didn't take it calmly. "What?" he screamed into the phone. "Exactly how bad is it?"

"Pretty bad," came the unwelcome reply. "We don't know how much data has been accessed," the techie said.

"What have you done to protect our client?" Charlie asked next, not relishing the prospect of explaining this to Jimmy the Juice.

"We have changed the encryption keys," he said, "but beyond that there is nothing we can do and still remain online. We could shut down the gaming sites for a while in order to regenerate the keys, but if they could break it before, they can do it again."

"Find out who's doing it, and call me back," Charlie ordered. "One of the beauties of the internet highway is it's a two-way street," he thought as he telephoned his lawyer, Walter Fulham QC.

Walter took the call on his cell phone as he was on his way to a political fund-raising dinner. "This could be of interest to the Committee which oversees the Center's operations," Walter said after Charlie finished his tirade about intrusive and irresponsible governments. "Not to mention the civil liberties people. You may not be able to win the battle, but the war is another thing."

That evening, Walter made sure he bent the ears of select politicians at the black tie affair. Judging by the shock waves that rippled through the evening, Walter was satisfied that he had made an impression.

"Democracy in action," he thought as he drove home. Tomorrow he would report to his client.

Closure

As the computer technician walked down the long hall for his hastily called meeting with John Blackmore in the Center for Internet Studies, he was feeling quite pleased with himself. He carried his file which contained chapter and verse on Jimmy the Juice and his involvement in True Blue Gaming.

"Sit down son, and shut the door," Blackmore said quietly from behind his desk. "I received a call from the Attorney General's office this morning telling me to drop the True Blue investigation," he said, raising his hand to stop the youth from voicing any objection.

"The matter is closed," Blackmore continued. "You will give

me all your files, erase your computer files, and forget this incident ever happened. Thank you for your help. That will be all," he said, showing him the door.

Charlie was delighted the right pressure had scored a victory for privacy, but less so about his meeting with Jimmy. "Do you think I'm stupid?" he started as Charlie squirmed in his chair.

"I don't like to be made a fool of," Jimmy hissed. "Now they know I'm connected with True Blue, which means we have to close it down. We both lose, and I don't like to lose. Bottom line, you owe me a favor which I plan to collect someday. You can go now."

15.

Whose Money is it Anyway?

November, 2001

> *"In general, the art of government consists in taking as much money*
> *as possible from one class of citizens to give to the other."*
>
> — Voltaire

The Department of Public Works was a great place to work. It existed between the Department of Finance, which collected tax revenues, and all the other departments, which spent the tax revenues (and frequently more). Awash in all that money resulted in slippage of huge proportions.

Nobody knew this better than Ed Smith, who had been a Second Assistant Deputy Minister for over five years. He ran his personal government surplus program, which he justified in a number of ways. First, he was paid a salary way below his abilities. Next, everybody who could did the same. And last, nobody ever noticed or cared.

Plucking the Goose

The sheer apathy of the civil service lent an air of respectability to his side operations. "If they can't take a joke," Ed thought, "why should I care?"

Ed's mind returned to his early days as the child of a union activist when he learned why the little guy needed protection. Now he was in a position to do something about that.

His favorite memory of his job was about the day the requisition for twenty mountain bikes landed on his desk. They had been ordered by the Youth Enhancement Department in order to take underprivileged adolescents bicycle riding, away from their city slums.

What impressed Ed right off was the sheer cheek of his counterpart at the other ministry. The order was for fifteen-speed mountain bikes made of the finest procurable titanium and equipment at a cost of $2,300 each!

"Where are they planning to take these kids riding?" he thought. "While they're at it, why not charter a plane to airlift them and the bikes?"

Of course, the plane charter came under another ministry, so it was a rhetorical question. Ed Smith liked rhetorical questions because he could never be accused of having the wrong answer – one of the basic survival skills of the career civil servant.

By prearrangement with the other department, it was a simple matter to add four extra bikes. Instead of ordering twenty bikes, the forms were processed in quadruplicate for twenty-four. One week later, the funds were authorized, and another week after that twenty-four gleaming mountain bikes were delivered.

Two months later, three slightly used bikes were in Ed's garage (the fourth was at his cohort's home). Ed's children really liked those bikes; he scored a lot of brownie points with the family on that deal.

Finally Ed was in line for promotion to Assistant Deputy Minister. This was the most important position in the entire bureaucracy as it allowed him to allocate funding to nongovernment projects directly. No more merchandize to take in order to realize his cut.

Knowing he was a shoo-in for the position, the Deputy Minister had already given Ed two files to review. He was as torn as a dog between two fire hydrants as to which project to fund. One was a forgivable hotel loan in the Deputy Minister's riding. This alone recommended it as the better choice.

The hotel had been losing money for years, but employed a lot of people in a depressed area. Ed would share 10% of the loan proceeds with his boss and the applicant for the loan. Since the loan was for $600,000, he was already dreaming of ways to spend his third. $20,000 is a lot of money for a bureaucrat earning a paltry $78,000 per year.

The other file was to fund youth summer training programs. This application was also a good choice as nobody at the Youth Enhancement Ministry ever kept track of exactly where its money was spent. Quite how they accomplished this Ed could only guess.

At $2.3 Million, it was very tempting. For this project, Ed would have to split 5% with the Deputy and his counterpart due to the large size of the loan. He decided this was not a decision he should make alone, and called his Deputy Minster for a meeting.

Soaring with Eagles

The Deputy Minister's office was the typically spacious kind reserved for senior civil servants, furnished with uninspiring government-issue furniture (bought by Ed's Department many years before). Ed was ushered to the couch by the Deputy's secretary where tea and cookies waited on the coffee table.

The Deputy was finishing a telephone conversation with his Minister, the politician elected by the people and entrusted by the

Prime Minister with spending their money.

To be perfectly candid, everyone in the civil service operated on the basis it was their money, not the taxpayers. And they definitely knew it didn't belong to the politicians, who couldn't be trusted to know anything practical.

Government worked for one reason – an entrenched bureaucracy that never changed. They were the professionals who understood the pulse of the populace. They also knew how to allocate just enough funds to high profile projects to show the electorate its tax dollars at work. They were the ones who ensured the smooth continuity of government while politicians of different stripes came and went.

As the Deputy Minister sat down at the coffee table, Ed opened the two files. "Sir, first of all, may I say how grateful I am to be allowed the opportunity to assist you," he said. "I know I'm up to the task, and hope my promotion is favorably received."

"Have no fear, Ed," replied the Deputy Minister. "The word is you've already been approved. Only formalities remain." Ed breathed an audible sign of relief, and turned their attention to the files before them.

"To be honest," Ed began, "I'm having difficulty deciding which project to fund. They are both worthy causes, and..." He was cut short by the Deputy's question: "Why not fund both? The current Minister of Finance believes in high taxes and deficit budgets, so I don't see a problem."

"Very good," said Ed. "We'll start the paperwork right away." With that, he returned to his much smaller office and started assembling the team of bureaucrats necessary to marshal the large amount of documentation. By the time these loans were funded, the documents for each would fill several filing boxes. Ed knew how to paper a file to make it impervious to criticism.

Surrounded by Turkeys

A few days later, Ed was summoned to the Deputy's office, taking with him the two thickening files to show his progress. There was a somber tone to the office as he entered. The Deputy barely glanced at Ed as he waved him to a chair.

"Do you have a brother named Charlie?" the Deputy asked after a few seconds pause. As Ed nodded tentatively, he then asked "Is that the same Charlie Smith who owns Global Wealth Group, and has had numerous run-ins with the law, including being thrown in jail?" The Deputy's eyes were riveted to Ed's.

"You're a good man, Ed," the Deputy continued, "but this business with your brother precludes your elevation to ADM. We have to be so careful these days. I'm afraid it's out of my hands."

Then, using the protocol of managers worldwide, the Deputy put his hand gently on Ed's shoulder as he walked him out of his office and quietly shut the door. Dumbstruck, Ed found himself alone in the barren hallway, abandoned by his former mentor.

Later that day, and nursing his third Campari and soda at home, Ed resolved to call his brother. "They passed me over after doing a check on my family," he said. "I just can't believe it."

"Don't take it too hard," Charlie consoled him. "Let's have lunch next week when I'm in town, and see about arranging funding for an affiliate of the Global Wealth Group.

"We have a number of interesting projects on the go," continued Charlie. "I have no doubt that with your connections and expertise in preparing the files, we'll have little difficulty in reclaiming some of our money from their coffers. After all, what's family for?" Charlie asked, rhetorically.

16.

Terror at Charlie's Laundromat

January, 2002

"If a way to the better there be,
it lies in taking a full look at the worst."

— Thomas Hardy

Ali al Matraka's days usually followed a set routine – up at 5:00 a.m., prayers, breakfast followed by exercises until noon, prayers, lunch, read the daily newspapers, prayers, contact his cell leader at 3:15 p.m., small arms and demolition practice, prayers, supper, and finally sleep at 11:00 p.m.

He had been following this regimen faithfully almost every day since he arrived in his foster country and assumed his new identity seven years earlier.

Today everything had changed. He was on a city bus to meet his cell leader for the first time. Thirty minutes later, he entered the small café and approached the man wearing dark glasses sipping coffee at the corner table.

The Mission

"*Allah akbar,*" Ali said to the man, who replied "May Allah be victorious." The correct passwords exchanged, Ali sat down to receive instructions from his cell leader, whose name he would never know.

The stranger casually passed a folded newspaper across the table, and spoke softly to Ali. "Inside the paper is a bank draft and business card of a man you are to visit tomorrow. He does not know who you are. He will ask you for identification, so you must use your forged documents.

"The bank draft is for $15 Million payable to the man's company," continued the cell leader. "You will tell him you represent an investment group, and you want to set up an offshore structure and transfer the funds to a brokerage account he recommends.

"Then you will wait ten days for the draft to clear," the cell leader said. "On the eleventh day, you will see him again, and instruct him to buy the following stocks on the basis you believe the stock market has stopped falling and the time is right to invest."

The two men talked about the details of the stocks, which Ali committed to memory. When they finished, the cell leader concluded by saying: "We will not speak again until I contact you to sell the stocks and transfer the funds. Now go, and don't look back. May Allah be with you."

Ali returned to his shabby apartment, drew the curtains and removed the bank draft and business card from the newspaper. He then telephoned Global Wealth Group and arranged to see Charlie Smith at 10:00 a.m. the next day. That done, he resumed his daily routine.

The Set-up

"Mr. Smith," said Miriam, Charlie's receptionist, "there's a Mr.

Matraka here to see you." Charlie went out to the reception area to greet his new prospect.

"Good morning Mr. Matraka," Charlie said. "Please come this way to my office where we can talk privately." Charlie liked to waste no time in reassuring clients he was entirely on their side. "Can I offer you coffee?"

"Thank you, no," Ali replied softly, disdaining this infidel who was trying to befriend him.

"Now, how can we help you?" Charlie asked as they sat down.

"I understand you specialize in protecting your clients' financial interests offshore," Ali said. "I represent a consortium of investors which has authorized me to put $15 Million into the stock market. For this I need an offshore structure and an offshore brokerage account."

"Then you have come to the right place," Charlie replied with delight. "In order to discharge our due diligence procedures, we will need to take a copy of your passport, which we will keep in the strictest confidence naturally.

"We can provide you with a corporate structure and an offshore investment account that will suit your needs. The funds will be banked offshore, away from prying eyes," Charlie finished with the characteristic twinkle in his eye.

"What is your fee structure?" Ali asked next, as he placed his forged passport and the bank draft on the desk.

Charlie looked at the bank draft as he answered. It was drawn on an Eastern bank he had never heard of. "$25,000 for the set-up, 1% annual management fee, both payable in advance, and normal brokerage rates for the trades."

"That will be acceptable," Ali replied. "When will the account be ready?"

"In eight days," Charlie said, and the meeting ended with the usual pleasantries. "Charlie," he said to himself, "today is most definitely your day." Then he sat back at his desk to revise his upcoming holiday budget.

Ten days later Ali returned to Global Wealth Group. "Here is a list of stocks we wish you to purchase, and the dollar amounts for each," Ali said.

Charlie perused the list of twenty-eight public companies, and felt a familiar twinge at the back of his neck. "Mr. Matraka," he said, "may I say this is a most interesting investment strategy. Not that I mean to pry; it's just that we can be more effective if we understand your goals."

"Not a problem," Ali replied. "My investors believe the demand for bottled water is going to strengthen significantly."

Satisfied, Charlie relayed the instructions to his offshore broker, who duly executed the trades. The broker did not notice what Charlie had: all the stocks were major bottled water companies.

The Plan Unfolds

Two weeks later, a highly coordinated effort by Ali's unknown comrades contaminated ninety-seven of the major urban reservoirs worldwide. Predictably, this caused global panic as reports simultaneously poured in about the resulting illness and deaths. The very young, elderly and infirm were the hardest hit.

As the numbers grew and cities struggled to contain the health disaster, there was a run on bottled water, and their publicly traded stock soared. Predictably, so did Ali's offshore portfolio.

Days later, Ali called Charlie to sell all the positions. "All of it?" Charlie asked in amazement. Never before had a client invested so much, so fast, and then liquidated everything all at once.

"That's correct," Ali said. "Please tell your broker to send the money to the new banking coordinates which have just been faxed to you. We'd prefer the funds be wired tomorrow, and will pay any early settlement fees."

Consequences

The two secret servicemen who visited Charlie looked like Hollywood caricatures: tall, muscular, wearing dark suits and glasses. Only the earphones were missing.

"Charlie Smith, you're under arrest for conspiracy, terrorism and other charges yet to be laid," said one of the agents. Charlie found himself paralyzed, unable to resist, and was led away in handcuffs.

At the first opportunity, Charlie contacted his lawyer, Walter Fulham QC. Fulham quickly assessed the situation, and convinced Charlie to abandon one of his credos. Charlie rolled over on his client, telling all.

The secret service wasted no time in tracing the trades and the flow of funds. Using international laws, it froze whatever bank accounts it could. At the end of the day, some of the money was recovered as proceeds of crime. The bulk, however, was never found.

When they arrived at Ali's apartment, he was long gone. Using his real passport, he left his adopted country to join his comrades and continue his training for the holy war. His camp was financed for years to follow.

A case of bottled water arrived at Global Wealth Group two days later. Charlie's receptionist took it to the kitchen, and poured herself a drink. A few minutes later, Miriam appeared in Charlie's doorway.

"Excuse me, Mr. Smith," she said weakly, "but I don't feel at all well. In fact..." and she stumbled to the floor, unable to speak, her eyes wide and unfocused.

Charlie rushed Miriam to emergency where she was tested, treated and stabilized. She was lucky. "You never can be too careful these days," Charlie thought as he calmed himself with a whiskey and soda. (He was off water for the time being.)

But the nagging question remained: what could he or anyone really do to protect themselves from money laundering and terrorism?

17.

Sinking Ships of State

March, 2002

"Good government obtains when those who are near are made happy, and those who are far away are attracted."
— Confucius

"It's every man for himself! Abandon ship!" were the last words Charlie Smith heard before he awoke from his fretful nap. The vision of a global blockade by the big ships of the little ones still haunted him. "They can't hijack them all, can they?" he thought as he reached for the remains of his tropical punch.

Charlie had dozed off lying poolside at his rented beachfront villa. The disturbing dream bore little resemblance to his peaceful surroundings – the gentle breeze, swaying palm trees and azure blue water.

He chose this island because it was relatively inexpensive and quiet. It had somehow eluded the new offshore press, whose passion was to stir up controversy wherever and whenever they could.

"One might even say they have become instruments of those who seek global conformity and domination," Charlie mused. Never one to welcome attention, he was relieved to be out of their limelight.

sharp.

As Charlie rose to wade into the pool, he was distracted by the thunder of jet planes overhead. He looked up to see four fighters flying in tight formation.

"I wonder where they're from," he thought. "Probably exercises or one of those air shows."

Standing waist-deep in the cool water, Charlie next noticed what he thought might be ships on the horizon. Too small to identify, but he could tell there were a lot of them.

Charlie's concentration was interrupted by several large explosions which sounded like they came from the airport. He ran to the house, grabbed the binoculars, and focused on the armada that was inching closer.

"Bloody hell," he said aloud. "We're being invaded!"

Operation Titanic

"Put down the binoculars, and stand still," came a stern voice from behind Charlie. "Now Mr. Smith, kindly turn around very slowly," the voice continued, more gently.

Charlie turned to see two soldiers in fatigues with rifles at the ready, flanking a third man wearing a suit, dark glasses and an earphone. He recognized the man in the suit as John Blackmore, one of the secret service agents who detained him a few months earlier for helping Ali al Matraka profit from terrorism.

Matraka was part of a terrorist organization that poisoned urban water supplies worldwide, and then used Charlie's Global Wealth Group to sell shares of publicly-traded bottled water companies, whose stocks soared in the ensuing panic. The money was banked offshore, and most of it evaporated before the authorities arrived.

Charlie was escorted into the house, and seated opposite

Blackmore in the living room. The two soldiers stood watch at the front and patio doors.

"Let me explain what's going on, and why we're here," Blackmore said. Charlie, still shaken, was trying desperately not to let his eyes wander over to the hall table where some private client files lay unnoticed.

"For security reasons, I can't go into detail," Blackmore continued. "The bottom line is this island is presently occupied by a multi-national force, which controls all the essential services. The government ministers are under house arrest, and the local police are confined to their barracks. Casualties have been minimal..."

"And let's not have one more", thought Charlie nervously. Guns got his attention, and he was keenly aware of his precarious situation.

"We're here by virtue of new anti-terrorism laws which have been passed by most countries, although not by this island," Blackmore said. "This island chose instead to harbor certain elements of a global terrorist organization, which is where you come in."

John Blackmore paused, removing his dark glasses so Charlie could see his firm resolve. "One of the terrorists we believe to be here is your old friend, Ali al Matraka," he said with satisfaction. "Small world, isn't it?"

"What do you want me to do?" Charlie asked, the resignation clear in his voice. "Is there nowhere left to run or hide anymore?" he asked himself.

"Very little, really," Blackmore replied. "Our boys will be combing this island over the next few days, and as the noose tightens Matraka may try to contact you for help. Once he's captured, we'll need you to identify him.

"We'll be your guests until this is over," Blackmore continued, "and we'll need to connect some equipment to your telephones in case Matraka calls. We don't expect the operation to take more than one week.

"Oh, and another thing," Blackmore added as he got up. "One of us will be with you at all times. So if you're planning any meetings or parties, I suggest you cancel them now."

"Lovely," thought Charlie. "Of all the places to visit, I ended up in the middle of an international incident."

As they moved into the hall, Charlie positioned himself between Blackmore and the file folders. "Can I fix you a drink?" Charlie asked. Blackmore shook his head.

"Then I presume you won't mind if I pour one for myself?" Charlie asked to Blackmore's back as he headed for the front door. Again, he just shook his head.

Charlie quietly scooped up the files and casually carried them into the kitchen where he surreptitiously stuffed them into a bottom drawer. Returning drink in hand, and with nothing to do but wait, Charlie returned to the pool.

Mopping Up

The next six days passed painfully slowly, punctuated by newscasts consisting of typical military statistics. The death toll stood at nineteen, mostly foreigners with Arab-sounding names. The reports, broadcast by the occupying forces, claimed the casualties belonged to one terrorist group or another.

Then the news broke that the island's Prime Minister had been shot and killed resisting arrest. It was well known he did not support the new suspension of individual freedoms and the anti-terrorist sentiment that led to the invasion of his country. What proved fatal were his politics had the wrong political stripe.

"What is the future of statehood when political leaders are summarily removed by foreign forces which no longer tolerate opposition?" Charlie asked himself, looking down at the troubled Paradise from his airplane as he headed home.

Plugging the Leaks

Ali al Matraka never was found, nor anyone for that matter who could be linked to his terrorist group, both to Charlie's amusement and relief.

Over time, the questions circling the invasion "of titanic disproportion" as one reporter put it died down, amid innuendo that the casualties and prisoners all had legitimate reasons to be on the island.

Particularly embarrassing was a group of six men identified as being laborers imported four months earlier to repair a hotel damaged by a hurricane. Apparently they attracted attention by wiring their salaries home to help feed and clothe their families.

In a futile effort to justify the invasion, still further reports suggested the late Prime Minister was up to no good. Not surprisingly, these were reinforced by the new Prime Minister who was installed by the provisional military government.

With all the spins in the news coming from the government players, the press was unable to discern what really happened. The stories contained so much contradictory information that the world eventually lost interest.

In no time at all, island life returned to normal. The islanders fished and entertained the trickle of curious tourists who were brave enough to defy the travel advisories issued by their governments.

The island's new government lavishly spent the aid it received from those same governments, eager to garner popular support. The damage to the airport and other public monuments was repaired, and the surviving prisoners were either released or deported as undesirable. The tiny tempest was thus safely contained.

As for Charlie, he arrived late at his office to find a note on his desk. His secretary had booked an appointment for him to see a new client who wanted to start a bank in the Middle East.

"Oh brother," Charlie muttered. "What next?"

18.

Doing As They Say

May, 2002

"Big Brother is watching you!"
— George Orwell

"What makes a country?" Charlie Smith asked his lawyer, Walter Fulham QC, over cocktails. The last few years had been stressful for Charlie, what with his being arrested twice, forced to assist the secret service invade a foreign state, being fired by his offshore bank, narrowly saving his receptionist from being poisoned by terrorists, not to mention the ongoing attack by the big countries against international banking.

These and other events had focused Charlie's mind on the bigger picture, particularly the changes to international relations and cooperation.

"More precisely," he continued, noticing Fulham's blank stare, "since countries are all about borders and self-determination, why should one country enforce the laws of another?"

"If we're going back to political science 101, I'd better order us some doubles," Fulham replied, catching the waiter's eye. "The world is shrinking fast. Thanks to computerization, satellite communication and cheap transportation, people now know everyone's business instantly.

sharp.

"So do our governments, who like to measure and compare everything," Fulham said. "And since the business of today's bureaucrats is to be nosy, they've discovered there is a common benefit from sharing information with their counterparts."

"Lovely," said Charlie, playing with his swizzle stick. "Then *1984* can't be far off. When do you suppose they'll decide to have a world government and centralize all the important powers, like information, so they can really keep us in line?"

"All governments know the value of propaganda to influence the attitude and behavior of their people," Fulham retorted.

"No question," interrupted Charlie. "Just like Orwell's phony war when Big Brother kept announcing statistics about the war that wasn't happening, simply to manipulate popular opinion."

"You don't honestly think it will go that far?" Fulham asked rhetorically, or maybe not, as he was about to find out from Charlie over the next hour.

The Real World

While Charlie and Walter were waxing philosophical in the pub, John Blackmore at the secret service was putting the final touches to his latest plan, which he code-named "Operation Shepherd". Blackmore had been assigned the task of using the newly enhanced anti-money laundering laws to "re-align" a certain small island nation.

Some months earlier, this sovereign state, or so it thought, democratically passed aggressive laws to attract foreign capital. These included guarantees of bank secrecy, no income tax and anonymous ownership of companies and trusts.

As a fledgling offshore financial center, it quickly caught the attention of the big boys, those countries that basically control world commerce. "Not a smart move," thought Blackmore as he called his superiors for the usual rubber stamp before swinging into action. That done, he contacted his computer techies at the Center for Internet Studies, the clandestine arm of the secret service.

"What we need," explained Blackmore to the two guys from the computer department, "is airtight evidence of criminal proceeds going to this country so we can lean on them to change their ways."

"No problem," replied the senior technician. "We have black programs in place that can show movement of funds from any criminal organization you choose, through numerous banks, to the final destination. How much money are we talking about?"

"I would say around $10 Million should do it," Blackmore said.

"Fine. Then what I'd suggest," continued the techie, "is we wire transfer the funds from our offshore bank through two more offshore banks who won't ask any questions, to the target country. We'll take care of the paperwork at our end. Just make sure you set up the last bank."

Operation Shepherd

Three days later, John Blackmore walked into Prime Bank and Trust, a medium-sized bank on the wayward island. It was located in a wooden building that had seen better days.

"If the termites stop holding hands," Blackmore muttered as he walked in, "the whole place will collapse."

Within thirty minutes, he found the employee he was looking for – underpaid, passed over for promotion twice with a growing family to feed.

After an evening of wining and dining the bank officer, and the promise of $1,000, Blackmore returned to the bank the next morning to open the account for his "clients" and pay the bribe.

Back in his hotel room, Blackmore made the calls to arrange the transfer of funds, which would not be questioned by the bank. His man assured him of this, eager to collect a second $1,000 once the funds were posted to the account.

Another few days and the stage was set. Blackmore arrived for his meeting with Prime Minister Cecil Drake, arranged through official channels. Blackmore was upbeat, confident his mark was unprepared for the trap he was about to spring.

"Good morning, sir," Blackmore said, presenting his credentials to Drake. An impressive man, the Prime Minister hadn't got where he was by being anyone's fool. He immediately noticed Blackmore was more than he appeared – too polished; something hidden behind those dark eyes...

"And to you, Mr. Blackmore," Drake replied. "What can we do for you today?"

The two men faced each other across Drake's desk, as Blackmore proceeded to lay out the evidence which showed conclusively that Prime Bank had received funds from one of the world's most notorious crime groups.

Letting the facts sink in, Blackmore paused a few moments before he let the penny drop.

"I'm sure you will agree, Prime Minister," Blackmore said, "that we have to crack down on international crime. We trust we can rely on your government to enact the model legislation that other countries have adopted."

"This is most distressing," Drake replied, still scanning the documents. "But tell me, what measures are the large countries, such as yours, taking to stop this so-called money laundering? It is common knowledge that most of this money goes through your banks, not ours. Only a small, some might say even insignificant, portion touches our shores." His eyes were now fixed on Blackmore, searching for a reaction.

"Quite frankly, sir," Blackmore replied, "you can't fight this. Stopping money laundering is our new priority. What we do is not your concern; what we say is. We trust we can expect your full cooperation." The tone of his voice left no doubt this was no request.

"So, Mr. Blackmore," Drake said, "it appears we have no real choice in this matter."

"I'm sure you will agree, sir," Blackmore said, "that it is in everyone's interest to get onto the same page and work together to rid the world of this scourge. Your nation stepped out of line with these secrecy laws. Now it's time to step back."

A perceptive man, Drake recognized he had no other option. He and his little country were just pawns in a much bigger game he would never fully understand. He dutifully took the pledge for conformity, in the best interest of his people.

"I wonder if the citizens of our little island country will agree I have done the right thing?" thought Drake. "Will they even care?"

The Last Word

The next day, Charlie read in the newspaper that the small island nation announced it was amending its banking laws to conform to the model legislation in widespread use.

A quotation from the Prime Minister vehemently denied his country had done anything wrong, stated the banking laws had been misinterpreted, but as a good world citizen they were repealing the offending laws in the interests of global harmony.

"I may not have many bowling pins left standing in my alley," Charlie told himself, "but I know pressure when I see it. Chalk up another casualty of globalization."

As for Blackmore, he returned home to find his young children climbing the walls and his wife frazzled. Moving swiftly to restore order in the house, he barked, "Children, behave yourselves!" When they didn't pay any attention to him, he yelled even louder, "Do as I say, right now, or face the consequences..."

19.

The War on Cash

July, 2002

"Farewell the plumed troop and the big wars,
that make ambition virtue!"

— Shakespeare

Having bagged two victories in a row, John Blackmore was something of a hero at the secret service. "Nice run; try to keep it up," his boss said. The latent threat was not lost on John. He knew he was only as good as his last kill, figuratively speaking of course. Who was to be his next target?

While Blackmore worked up his next mission, Charlie Smith was at the executive airport arranging a charter flight offshore. With his usual luck, he found himself assigned a rather jovial pilot with an unsettling sense of humor.

"Since we will be flying to an island," asked Charlie, "may I ask if your plane lands on water?"

"Yes it will, but only once," replied the pilot motioning to the twin engine, six-seater plane sitting on the tarmac. Charlie noticed the absence of pontoons and groaned inwardly. He was a nervous flier at the best of times, and his imagination was conjuring up all manner of horrible things that might happen.

As they walked to the plane, Charlie ventured another

sharp.

question: "I notice the plane has two engines; will it still fly with only one?"

"It will, but I have found that passengers find the rotating plane disquieting," replied the pilot to Charlie's rising distress.

The first thing Charlie located as he seated himself was the air sickness bag.

Charlie chose a private charter because he was bringing a large suitcase full of cash to a small island bank. This bank was one of the few which still accepted large quantities of currency in the wake of the rising global regulation designed to track everyone's movements.

Although no final statistics were published on the government crackdown against money laundering, Charlie rather suspected they would be equivocal. He highly doubted the bureaucratic approach could ever effectively curb criminal cunning, which always seemed to stay a few steps ahead, and be very adaptable.

"Unless they close down commerce altogether," thought Charlie as he tossed back two motion sickness pills, "and make us all employees of the state. Karl Marx would surely approve." The irony of this brought a faint smile to Charlie's pale lips.

Tropical Banking

Forcing his legs to move, Charlie barely managed his way through the enhanced immigration and customs hassles. He was a little apprehensive about getting the cash through, but a $200 tip convinced the pilot to carry in the case as his own. Pilots were still rarely checked.

Charlie finally arrived at his hotel at 4:15 p.m. Although a tiny island, having lowered import tariffs on cars a few years earlier, it now enjoyed traffic jams that rivaled the largest cities of the world.

Too late to go to the bank, it dawned on Charlie that the case of cash was too big for both the hotel safe and the safety deposit box in his room. He sat on the bed to sort out this dilemma and concluded he had only two choices: either keep the bag with him or hide the cash in the room.

"But where?" he asked himself as he scanned the room. "If I take it with me, I could be robbed or forget it somewhere. On the other hand, there is no place to hide it here."

Charlie was starting to get agitated when it hit him: rent a car and put the case in the trunk overnight. Which is exactly what he did and, feeling very pleased with himself, he adjourned to the hotel bar and grill for a relaxing evening.

A Chilly Reception

Charlie arrived at the bank at opening time and asked to see the managing director. "I'm very sorry, sir," replied the teller, "but he is off island all week."

"Then may I see his assistant?" asked Charlie with a familiar sense of foreboding.

"The assistant manager is traveling with him," continued the teller in a sing-song voice. "The compliance officer, Mrs. Frost, is here; would you like to speak with her?"

"But I had an appointment!" replied Charlie, not yet grasping the futility of his predicament. "Very well, Mrs. Frost will have to do," he said as he sat down to wait.

Josephine Frost appeared from an office in the back of the bank twelve minutes later. Charlie knew this because he was furiously watching his watch the whole time. His fury melted away as he watched her approaching him.

She was a tall, striking woman of African descent in her early thirties. She moved with a characteristic and very attractive rhythm.

"I apologize for the wait, Mr. Smith," she said, "but I just finished a meeting which went longer than expected." Charlie looked past her to see John Blackmore emerging from the same office, walking towards them.

"Hello Charlie," Blackmore said with perverse delight. "What a coincidence we should meet here. What's in the bag?" he asked, looking down at Charlie's suitcase.

"Oh, just clothes and personal effects," replied Charlie hastily. "I'm leaving the island directly from the bank."

"Really," said Blackmore. "I guess you are a busy man these days, what with all the new laws that affect your business."

Charlie wisely resisted the temptation to say what he really thought of this pompous bureaucrat and his misguided mission against international finance. "You have no idea," he replied instead, and moved off with Mrs. Frost to her tiny office in the back of the bank.

Frozen Cash

"Mr. Smith," said Mrs. Frost as she seated herself across from Charlie. "You don't really have your clothes in that suitcase, do you."

"Not necessarily," Charlie replied cautiously.

"I see," she continued. "That man you were just talking to, who seems to know you, is from the secret service. He is part of a special project with our government to detect money laundering.

"Mr. Smith, I don't want to know what is in your case," Mrs. Frost said. "If I even suspect it's cash, I will have to freeze the funds and file a suspicious transaction report with the financial crimes unit. In all likelihood that will be the last you'll see of the money.

"I'm telling this for your own good," she added, "because you are a customer of the bank. But my hands are tied. Our government has just frozen all accounts with more than $1 Million. If these people cannot establish a legitimate source of funds, they will forfeit them. Our own Director of Customs has $5 Million frozen is his account."

"So the War on Drugs is now the War on Cash," Charlie muttered as he looked despondently at his suitcase. A chill ran though his body, making him shiver. While the managing director was compliant, the compliance officer was anything but.

Capital Flight

What happened next was exactly what John Blackmore and his handlers intended. Charlie Smith tried to leave the country, and was caught with his case of cash by the airport authorities.

"What do you mean, I can't take my belongings with me?" Charlie demanded, his voice in high pitch. But it was no use, as he well knew. The times had changed, clearly evidenced by the blank stares from the customs officials circling him and his suitcase.

Charlie was shown into the side room (to avoid upsetting the tourists) and his suitcase was opened, revealing the money.

"Mr. Smith," the customs officer said, "under the new legislation, we must confiscate these funds. You have thirty days to file a report on where this money came from, or it will go to the government."

Not having a ready response, Charlie decided to depart and return another day for the cash. Which he didn't do, for two very good reasons: he couldn't establish a credible source for the funds;

and he did not want to experience the government's penal hospitality.

The deadline passed, and Charlie's cash was transferred to the government by operation of the new law. Through a complex series of transactions, however, it found its way to a new private account off island of the Director of Customs.

"One cannot be too careful anymore," Charlie mused as he read the bank confirmation.

Little did he know that an apoplectic John Blackmore was hot on the trail, still smarting from the reprimand by his boss for letting the seized money slip through his fingers.

20.

The Second Great Lie

September, 2002

"The potential for the disastrous rise of misplaced power exists and will persist."

— Dwight D. Eisenhower

Of the things Charlie Smith avoided doing in life, near the top of his list was going to movies with his grandchildren. Standing in line for the latest kids' show with his three grandkids and their little friends, he tried not to ask himself questions like "What am I doing here?"

Instead he concentrated on the line that snaked towards the ticket booth, calculating the time it took each customer to order, pay for and receive tickets.

"At this rate," Charlie said optimistically to no one in particular, "we may be too late to see the show."

"No problem Gramps," replied his grandson looking up at him. "We can always see the other movie which starts fifteen minutes later."

As Charlie cringed at being called "Gramps", he realized they were at one of those multiple cinemas that featured six different movies. He was trapped, moving slowly but relentlessly towards two hours of...

sharp.

Showdown

"Which show and how many tickets?" asked the disinterested teenager inside the glass booth. Charlie looked down at the small crowd around him and took a head count. Regrettably all of them were present and accounted for.

"That'll be one adult and five children," he said.

"$54.50 please," came the unwanted reply from the cashier who was busy studying her computer screen. Charlie opened his wallet and pushed a $100 bill through the wicket.

"I'm sorry sir," she said, finally looking at him. "We cannot accept $100 bills. Do you have anything smaller?" Her recital of the training manual was flawless. Charlie barely resisted the temptation to offer her one of the children as payment in kind.

"Are you saying you do not accept the official and legal currency of our country?" Charlie asked, using his most incredulous voice.

"We've had too many fake $100 bills," the girl replied unsympathetically. "The company doesn't take them anymore."

"I might understand if I were buying something for a few dollars," Charlie said, getting into his stride, "but these tickets are costing me almost $100, which you won't accept! How, pray tell, am I supposed to pay for the popcorn and drinks if I give you all my change?"

"You can pay by credit card," the cashier replied unfazed. This left Charlie in a corner with only two ways out: he could either inform the children they were leaving and suffer the unthinkable consequences; or pay with his credit card.

Retreating discreetly, Charlie signed the credit card voucher. The group proceeded to the concession stand where Charlie grumbled through the same routine with the same results.

While Charlie was challenging theatrical monetary policy at home, John Blackmore of the secret service was keeping an appointment several thousand miles away.

As Blackmore waited for his host to appear, he looked around at the sumptuous villa with its rambling tropical gardens. He sipped the iced tea given to him by the starched servant, and noted the perfect temperature and pleasing melodies from the exotic birds. Not a bad set up in a country generally labeled Third World.

Pedro Ramirez Gonzalez, alias "the Barracuda", entered the room with a flourish. He was every inch the Latin dandy – slick black hair, neat moustache, smoldering *Presidente* cigar perched on his right hand.

"Señor Blackmore," the Barracuda said with mock hospitality. "How interesting to finally meet you. After my last encounter with your government, I did not expect to have this pleasure."

"Globalization creates unusual alliances, don't you think Mr. Ramirez?" replied Blackmore cryptically. "I have a business proposition which is both suited to a man of your unique talents and mutually rewarding."

"*Gracias señor* ", said the Barracuda nodding his head. "I'm sure we can talk as men of the world. Continue *por favor.*"

"As you know," Blackmore explained, "my government is dedicated, along with many other major countries, to stopping the flow of criminal proceeds. The new focus on money laundering has vastly expanded our powers but, quite frankly, has also created an accounting nightmare.

"It's no secret that without widespread computerization and the internet," Blackmore continued, "we'd be unable to track the myriad financial transactions and detect money laundering with any degree of success. And now that we have the offshore countries and banks on the run, we should see some interesting results in the near future.

"This is where you come in, Pedro," Blackmore said. "The use of cash directly conflicts with our mandate since we can't follow it. Cash breaks the chain of transactions. Our next priority is to discredit the use of cash and persuade people to use credit cards and other traceable bank transactions. That way we can watch their every move."

"*Perdón señor*", Ramirez interrupted, "but I fail to see how I can assist you in this matter."

"Quite simply, really," Blackmore replied. "The phony currency in circulation is small potatoes. We need a large scale, organized counterfeiting operation to get everyone's attention.

"I have in my possession plates for printing the best forged $100 bills currently available. We will lend you these plates, give you the paper and ink, and you will use your organization to circulate the forgeries. The amount will be significant, and will make you a great deal of money."

"I fully understand the profit for me and my associates, but you said your proposal would be *mutually* rewarding," said the Barracuda, inviting Blackmore to name his share of the take.

"The profits are entirely yours to keep," answered Blackmore, to the Barracuda's surprise. "Our reward will be your success, which will help us convince people that cash is no longer viable."

"Señor Blackmore," said a notably impressed Barracuda. "You are truly devious; it will be an honor to work with you."

Fallout

In one of those ironic twists of today's increasingly complex politics, Charlie Smith found his cash increasingly unacceptable courtesy of the very government that issued the notes.

This presented a real problem for Charlie and his offshore business, since the banks had been turned into fiscal policemen, eliminating the bond of privacy with their customers. It was becoming painfully clear to Charlie and his clients that their governments were intent on knowing everything.

Returning to his office, John Blackmore was intercepted by his secretary. "Number One wants to see you about Operation Pandora immediately," she said solemnly. "He sounded very growly. Good luck."

As Blackmore walked past Number One's secretary, he noticed she avoided eye contact. Not a good sign.

"I hear you've been a bad boy, yes?" barked Number One at Blackmore who stood at attention before him.

"Excuse me, sir?" Blackmore asked in reply, eyes forward, looking nowhere in particular.

"Don't play the innocent with me, Johnny-boy," came Number One's instant response. Blackmore's boss was not to be trifled with. A former Army General, he could verbally kill a man at twenty paces. "The Minister of Finance was just here, jumping up and down about your operation destabilizing his currency!"

"With the greatest respect, sir. Isn't this all about the second great lie?" Blackmore asked as evenly as he could muster.

"I beg your pardon?" One replied more quietly, both confused and curious. In truth, Blackmore was one of his best field men.

"You remember sir," Blackmore answered with the slightest cynical smile. "The one where I say: ' I'm from the government, and I'm here to help you.'"

21.

An Arresting Affair

November, 2002

"Men are most apt to believe what they least understand."
— Montaigne

Sitting with assorted relatives at his nephew's wedding, Charlie Smith kept thinking something was not quite right. Maybe it was the fact his side of the party occupied one table, while the bride's party took up thirteen tables.

Perhaps it was the pricey jewelry dripping from the stunning women in the latest haute couture. Or the impeccably dressed men with their black hair slicked back.

They certainly knew how to party, dancing up a storm to Latin songs Charlie had never heard. He also didn't know the exotic dances, something he had in common with the others at his table since no one was venturing onto the dance floor. They just sat there and watched in collective disbelief.

Maybe it was because nobody had approached their table to introduce themselves. The glamorous side was keeping to itself. Charlie was merely an onlooker at a gala affair imported from Latin America.

Charlie's new niece, Isabella Maria Conchita Fernandez, was Colombian, presumably like her guests who flew in for the wedding. She was a sight to behold with her raven hair, her dark skin setting off her white gown and the emerald and diamond necklace. Charlie watched as she flashed her large brown eyes and favored all suitors with a dance apiece.

The lovely Isabella was in marked contrast to Charlie's nephew, Ernie, a forty-two year old, short, balding, airline mechanic of modest intellect and prospects. Ernie had the same job for the last twelve years; about the best thing you could say was he was a trusted and loyal worker.

Too Good to be True

"It just doesn't add up," Charlie thought, not one to readily accept that true love conquers all. At long last the music changed to a Louie Armstrong tune that Charlie recognized:

> "Sittin' in the sun
> Countin' my money,
> Fanned by the summer breeze.
> Sweeter than honey
> Is countin' my money,
> Those greenbacks on the trees."

As he listened to Sachmo grind out the familiar lyrics, Charlie was momentarily transported to Easy Street where the sun always shines, the house is paid for, and the back yard never needs weeding. When Louis Armstrong recorded *Sittin' in the Sun* on July 16, 1953, the world was a different place. Times were simpler, as were people's hopes and expectations. So too was the relationship with their governments. In 1953 there was only a handful of tax havens; now there were over sixty (and still countin').

shaup.

Then Charlie noticed the change in music signaled a new phase in the festivities. Everyone was returning to their seats as the bride's father announced something from the podium. Next the bride and groom started going table to table with a large cardboard box. Charlie could hardly believe his eyes. People were opening their wallets and purses and dropping cash into the box. And not just any cash, but thousands of dollars!

Before Charlie was able to escape to the washroom, Ernie and Isabella were at his table, box outstretched, while her father asked for donations to help them start their new life. Charlie shakily leafed through his wallet only to find an inadequate supply of bills.

"Will a cheque be alright?" Charlie asked sheepishly to bellowing laughter from the father-in-law.

"Provided it is a good cheque, *señor*," he replied with a wink. Charlie felt like crawling under the table; instead he searched his jacket pockets for his chequebook.

"Will you look at that," Charlie said. "I don't seem to have my chequebook with me. I'll send one along to Ernie tomorrow." That seemed to satisfy them, and they moved off to touch the next table.

Easy Street

Months passed before Charlie saw his nephew again. During that time, Ernie and Isabella made four trips to Colombia to visit her family. On each visit numerous gifts were lavished on the newlyweds.

"I can't tell you how lucky I am, Charlie," Ernie said to his uncle over lunch in the airport cafeteria. "Isabella is like a dream come true. We agree on almost everything. The only thing is she doesn't want any children. But she'll come around in time."

"You certainly seem to be very happy," Charlie replied. "I'm curious about the many presents you mentioned. What sort of things do they give you?"

"You know, that's a funny thing," Ernie said. "I honestly have no idea. Isabella gets all the boxes and takes care of them when we get home. I guess it's mostly crystal, jewelry – you know, stuff for Isabella and the house." There was a pause as Ernie looked thoughtfully nowhere in particular.

"Actually, they did give me a silk shirt on our first trip," Ernie added. "But Isabella handled the rest. I never thought to ask."

"It must cost you a fortune in customs duties," Charlie said.

"Not at all," Ernie answered. "They all know me at the airport, so I go through the crew entrance. I never get checked, and it costs me nothing."

If Ernie didn't see what has happening, Charlie's sixth sense was on full alert. The only problem was his nephew was too love-struck to listen to reason. He had a gorgeous wife from Colombia who was importing boxes, containing what? What were the chances they were household trinkets? "Not bloody likely," Charlie muttered to himself.

"Pardon me; did you say something?" Ernie asked.

"Oh, nothing," Charlie said. "Tell me, do you and Isabella travel together on these trips?"

"We did the first time," Ernie said. "The other three trips she stayed on longer. Anyway, I had to get back to work."

"So you brought the packages back alone," Charlie said, hoping his nephew would clue in.

"That's right," Ernie replied. "Isabella wouldn't be allowed through the crew gate. It's much easier for me to bring the presents home alone."

"And you've never opened any of the boxes?" Charlie asked.

"Not one," Ernie said. "As I said before, they're all presents for Isabella."

Dire Straits

Ernie thought nothing more about his uncle's questions as he continued his trips with Isabella. Returning home from his tenth trip, he was unexpectedly stopped by a customs officer.

"Excuse me, Mr. Smith," he said to Ernie. "I need to ask you a few questions. Please come with me." He led Ernie to an interrogation room where he was surprised to find his luggage open and being inspected by another officer.

"Do you know what's in these boxes?" asked one of the customs officers.

"No I don't," Ernie replied. "They're gifts to my wife who is still in Colombia. We could call her if you like."

"That won't be necessary," the agent said as they opened the boxes one by one, revealing $800,000 in cash neatly banded in $10,000 packets. The astonished look on Ernie's face told the officers everything. He still didn't get it.

"Please have a seat, Mr. Smith," the agent said motioning him to the nearest chair. "You were seen by one of our operatives in Colombia with Ricardo Fernandez, one of the biggest drug lords in the country. He did some checking and discovered you were making regular trips there. Then he called us to intercept you on your return.

"This cash is undoubtedly drug money," the agent continued, "and you are being used by your wife and her father to launder it. Do you have any idea where the other cash is now?"

"No," Ernie said despondently. "Other than the $100,000 we got at our wedding, which we used to pay off our mortgage, I haven't seen any other money. Isabella dealt with all that. I was busy at my job here."

The speed with which Ernie's life unraveled was dizzying. The good news was the authorities accepted he had been duped, so no jail time. However, they took his house away as proceeds of crime, and Ernie lost his job since he was deemed untrustworthy. The lovely Isabella filed for divorce.

Back at the Fernandez hacienda, Señor Fernandez consoled Isabella. "You are truly a loyal daughter," he said. "You have earned the respect of our entire family. The plan was masterful. And to think the cash that was seized amounted to only 10% – a most reasonable price to pay to put our money back in circulation."

22.

Donuts over Andros

April, 2003

"I might have been a goldfish in a bowl for all the privacy I got."
— Saki

Strapped into the co-pilot's seat of the six-seater plane, Charlie Smith was breathing deeply as he stared at the reassuring dials that promised him a safe flight. Since he was the only passenger, the pilot had him ride up front.

Charlie knew nothing about planes, loathed flying, and would have preferred to be practically anywhere else. But his global financial business demanded that he travel, and sometimes the best way to get to an offshore island was by small regional carriers.

The fact that the plane creaked, groaned and was held together in spots by duct tape only added to Charlie's anxiety.

"Donut?" asked the pilot as he handed Charlie the box, which he had to take because there was nowhere else to put it. Balancing the box on his lap, Charlie looked down at the Caribbean Sea. They were over a relatively large and sparsely populated island.

"What's that?" Charlie asked through the headphones.

"Andros," replied the pilot. "It's the largest island in The Bahamas, and..." His travelogue was cut short by the plane's call number being announced over the radio.

"Nassau Control, this is November, Foxtrot, Whiskey, Tango, Bravo," responded the pilot.

"Do you have a Charlie Smith on board?" the controller asked. Charlie sank into his seat, feeling decidedly trapped as he heard the pilot answer affirmatively.

Busted

"Switch to the following radio frequency and put him on," the controller continued. "We have his sister here who says there's a family emergency."

Before Charlie could protest that he had no sister, the pilot traded his headphones for Charlie's so he could talk to her.

"Hello Charlie," a sensual voice said from the other end. "Remember me?"

"How could I ever forget *you*, Victoria?" Charlie replied, their last encounter still fresh in his memory. How she artfully extracted from him the information she needed to solve her legal problems, then quietly disappeared, sending her thanks later by postcard.

Dear, lovely, devious Victoria – Charlie had to admire a woman like that.

"But how did you manage to call me here?" Charlie asked, still in shock.

"Quite simple, really," Victoria replied. "Your eye was scanned at the airport as you boarded, so the helpful people here had no difficulty placing you on the plane."

"And, where is *here*?" Charlie asked next, reminding himself not to underestimate her.

"On our island, of course," Victoria said. "I was hoping you might drop in."

As luck would have it, Charlie was heading to the spot where

Victoria was waiting, and arranged to meet her for cocktails. Then he returned his attention to keeping his nerves in check as the little plane droned and vibrated its way slowly over the vast sea dotted by the occasional island.

Nowhere to Run

Charlie entered the beachfront restaurant and found Victoria Cheethem sitting alone at a table for two.

"It's wonderful to see you again," Victoria said as he sat down, sliding a note across the table, which read:

We are being watched.
Meet me in 3 minutes in the parking lot.

Victoria excused herself and walked over to the powder room. As he sipped from his water glass, Charlie looked around but didn't see anything out of the ordinary.

A minute later, a different woman emerged from the restroom and left the restaurant. Then Charlie noticed a man in casual tropical clothes and dark glasses follow her out.

"Curious he should wear sunglasses at night," Charlie thought as he counted down the seconds. At precisely three minutes, he proceeded to the parking lot, and stood there alone waiting for his eyes to adjust to the dark.

Suddenly, two headlights turned on, and a sports car roared up to him, screeching to a halt.

"Get in!" barked Victoria from behind the steering wheel. Against his better judgment, Charlie jumped in, and they sped off into the night.

They drove for several minutes without talking. When Victoria was certain they weren't being followed, she spoke up: "I didn't want to take any chances we could be overhead. The dark glasses on that guy probably contain a parabolic microphone. He's been following me for days," she said.

Charlie had heard about some new glasses that could eavesdrop on people's conversations, but hadn't given the implications much thought. "How do you know this car isn't bugged, or have a tracking device on it so he can find us?" he asked Victoria, who abruptly stopped the car beside a large expanse of beach.

"Shall we go for a walk in the moonlight?" Victoria asked, as if she hadn't a care in the world.

As they walked on the sand, Charlie kept looking back to the parked car to see if they had company. He saw and heard nothing, other than the waves crashing beside them.

Hiding in Plain View

"May I ask who is so interested in you, and why?" Charlie asked at length.

"I can only think it's something to do with my new home here," Victoria replied, looking out to sea. "Since our last meeting, I organized my affairs as you advised to protect my assets. I formed multiple legal structures using international companies, foundations, trusts and bank accounts. I did everything I could to eliminate any paper trail that led back to me.

"Four months ago I moved here and purchased a modest estate using a domestic company," Victoria continued. "The purchase money was wired to the company's lawyer. My name did not, and does not appear anywhere. I thought I was finally free of the ghosts from my past…until now."

BEWARE
OF DOG

sharp.

Charlie was as curious as a cat peering into a mouse hole. "What can this house possibly have to do with your being watched?" he asked.

"It's likely because of all the security equipment I imported," Victoria replied. "To ensure my privacy, I bought a full array of devices – an entrance system which scans your hand, motion activated cameras, infrared beams around the perimeter, and the like. I even installed three panic rooms, which also had to be imported."

"Victoria," Charlie said, "let nobody say your life is dull. You are doubtless familiar with the accounting principles called LIFO and FIFO. In the offshore world, we use LILO to keep our affairs away from prying eyes. You have obviously attracted someone's attention by bringing in all this sophisticated equipment.

"Government agents think there is no legitimate reason for being offshore," Charlie continued. "People with nothing to hide, they say, don't need privacy, since they have nothing to fear. The problem with this argument is that it conveniently overlooks human frailty. Since when did people in government become more honest than the rest of us? I know places where you can buy a corrupt official for a few hundred dollars.

"Freedom without privacy is like apple pie without apples," Charlie said. "But trying to hide behind the walls of your estate while the world watches doesn't give you privacy. It makes you a prisoner. Sometimes the best place to be alone is in a crowd of people, provided there aren't any surveillance cameras around."

"Then what do you think I should do?" Victoria asked after a long pause. Charlie smiled inwardly as he saw his chance to make up the loss Virginia caused him at their last encounter when she extracted the valuable advice she needed, and then left town without so much as a "hi-de-ho".

"I think you should invite me over to your place," Charlie replied with a rakish grin, "so we can consider your position more deeply."

Victoria's estate was grand by any standard, and loaded with gismos that whirred, blinked and otherwise tracked Charlie's every movement. After fully acquainting himself with every aspect of Victoria's assets, Charlie convinced her to transfer her affairs to his management company, and leave the island. She would disappear again, and resurface with an even lower profile elsewhere.

About a week later Charlie answered the door of Victoria's former home. A reluctant man wearing dark glasses introduced himself as being from the Ministry of Technology, and asked for the lady of the house.

When Charlie replied that she'd moved away, he was momentarily disappointed. Then he asked Charlie if he could look around, as he'd been trying to contact the owner for days for advice to improve the security at the Prime Minister's residence.

23.

The Dangerous Duck

October, 2003

"The truth is rarely pure, and never simple."

– Oscar Wilde

From the moment Charlie Smith set foot in the all-inclusive resort Victoria had chosen for their romantic getaway, he had misgivings. Victoria Cheethem, the new love of Charlie's life, had persuaded him they needed time away from their island Paradise. Somewhere they could be alone, anonymous and far from their regular lives.

Perhaps "regular" wasn't the most accurate description of their lives. What with Charlie's offshore consulting business that regularly took him to faraway places, mixing him up with all manner of scoundrels in unpredictable circumstances.

Victoria had her share of challenges too, as she stayed one step ahead of forces intent on separating her from her fortune, or ill-gotten gains as they would say.

Charlie doubted this getaway would make any difference, recalling the story of the man who took a vacation to get away from his many problems, only to find nothing improved as he had taken himself with him. The state of affairs which prompted this mini-vacation was a case in point.

Charlie was currently living in Victoria's secluded island mansion that most people could only dream about, but which Victoria couldn't use for fear she might be found. Meanwhile she was island-hopping, staying in budget hotels and paying cash to maintain a low profile.

An All-Exclusive Experience

This resort was their first time together in months, and a welcome taste of the luxury Victoria couldn't enjoy; or so they thought. While all-inclusive hotels offer the world, they can be short on delivery, and this one was no exception.

Reality began to set in when they walked down the hall to their room, having been duly wrist-banded like some endangered species so their movements could be tracked. It wasn't anything in particular, except the hallway was dark and dingy. And once in their room, the colors were drab inside and out. The grand dame was showing her age.

"Well, here we are," murmured Victoria as she put her arms around Charlie's neck. She was apparently less interested in the décor, which was good news all round for Charlie who decided he better make the most of their time together.

Over the course of the next week, Charlie would come to realize that the true meaning of "all-inclusive" is the never-ending buffet. There was literally food everywhere, all day long. They even had a midnight snack for those who couldn't sleep without a full stomach.

As long as you didn't mind eating yesterday's leftovers cleverly disguised as today's casserole, there was plenty of food, even if it was uninspired and repetitive.

Charlie didn't care much for the lengthy queues he faced

every time he wanted food or drink, and mourned the lack of poolside waiters to take his drink orders. "All-inclusive" excludes the profit motive to provide attentive service.

And try as he might, Charlie failed to get into the neighboring resorts since he lacked their distinctive wrist bands. He belonged to the wrong endangered species.

"Shall we have a look around?" Charlie asked after he and Victoria satisfied themselves the bed was adequate to their needs.

They strolled arm in arm down to the lobby where Charlie suddenly found himself alone, Victoria having disappeared into one of the many hotel shops. He continued on alone, redeemed his voucher for a pool towel, and set out in search of the hot tub.

Hot Pot

As luck would have it, there was just enough space for Charlie to squeeze into the hot tub. He hesitated when he saw there were already six people in there, until the very large man opposite encouraged him with a friendly "Come on in".

The others shifted their seats to make room for Charlie, who lowered himself ever so slowly into the steaming, bubbling, highly chlorinated water.

Having settled in with the other lobsters in the pot, Charlie took a look around. The hot tub was situated strategically with a clear view of the white beach and its palm trees, palapas, sun worshippers and the sparkling blue water beyond. The setting, at least, was world class.

Turning to the occupants' conversation, it was obvious they were strangers that happenstance had thrown together.

"Hi, my name's Leroy. What's yours, bro?" asked the linebacker seated across the tub. Before Charlie could answer,

Leroy continued with introductions. "That's Rosa to your right. She's a Countess from Spain who has an international line of fashions," he said, nodding his head toward a comely young woman beside Charlie, who flashed him intriguingly dark eyes that aroused more than his curiosity.

"Beside her is Wei Moi, who says she's a tax auditor but promised not to take notes," the self-designated host chuckled. Charlie shifted his gaze reluctantly to the exquisite Oriental woman next to Rosa, whose porcelain skin and delicate features made Charlie self-conscious just looking at her. She said nothing, just smiled demurely and averted her eyes, inviting the football player to make the next introduction.

"This is Manny to my left. He's a lawyer, but we let him in when he told us he was used to hot water," he said of the thin, balding man who was quietly studying Charlie. Manny was in his eighties and liked to conserve energy, which Charlie deduced when he barely flickered his eyelids in salutation.

"To your immediate left is Antoinette, who's only told us she's a government economist," continued Mr. Loquacious. Charlie turned his head to see a middle-aged woman whose eyes twinkled with a knowledge of the world and men that made him even more self-conscious.

"And to my right is Rasheed, who tells us he's a banker," he concluded, indicating a smiling man with little hair, wire glasses and exceptionally white teeth. Charlie smiled back, unsure of what he'd stepped into as conversation resumed.

Bubble, Boil and Trouble

"The point I was trying to make," said Rasheed, "is that too much power has been ceded to bureaucrats who wield quasi-legal powers in place of the courts."

"I couldn't agree more," added Manny. "The expansion of government has supplanted the due process of law, and undermined the protection of an independent judiciary which are cornerstones of democracy."

"*Mes chers*," said Antoinette to the men present, "while your defense of *la liberté* is admirable, you must acknowledge the stability that a continuous civil service brings to the state. *Par exemple*, the financial disaster caused to the industrial nations by the rogue offshore states a few years ago would not have occurred if they had been properly regulated."

Charlie felt himself sinking into the water, as if to dodge shrapnel. Too late; Rasheed took the bait. "Are you seriously suggesting," Rasheed retorted, "that a world policed by bureaucrats is improving it?"

"Señor Rasheed makes an excellent point," interjected Rosa. "I have quite enough red tape already as *mi compañia* tries to accommodate the diverse rules of the different countries where we sell our designs. Many of the rules do not make sense half the time. And dealing with the taxes is *mui* expensive," she added to Wei Moi beside her.

"If you please," Wei Moi responded softly since everyone was now looking at her. "While my current role is to enforce tax laws, when I retire to private practice I shall be working actively to avoid them, so in this sense I support complex regulations since they provide me with a living."

"Let's everybody simmer down," said Leroy, extending his giant hands as if to calm the water. "I don't know about you, but all I want to do is play ball and pay my taxes. What's so wrong with that?"

You could have knocked the rest of them over with a feather, as they stared back at Leroy, their jaws open and speechless. While Leroy retreated by saying "What? What?", Charlie couldn't help but reflect that he was in a microcosm of the world that was about to boil over.

If this group of affluent and intelligent hotel guests couldn't see eye to eye in this all-inclusive and highly regulated environment, how could people be expected to agree in the real world?

As Charlie started to extricate himself from the cauldron, pink and ready to serve, Rosa asked plaintively: *"Por favor, Señor,* must you go so soon?" He made his excuses as simply as he could, but not without giving up both his name and occupation.

Charlie made his way back to the pool kiosk, and was exchanging his soggy towel for the voucher when he felt a gentle tap on his shoulder, and looked back to see Rasheed.

"Mr. Charlie," said Rasheed, "I was wondering if we could meet tomorrow at, say, one o'clock in the marina to discuss some items of mutual interest." Charlie readily agreed, and watched as Rasheed scurried back to the hot tub to rejoin his steamy new friends.

As Charlie went in search of Victoria in the consumer jungle, he made a mental note about hot tubs: you find new clients in the damndest places.

Good Intentions

As agreed the day before, Charlie walked from his resort into the small marina attached to his resort at one o'clock. He found Rasheed Khalaffi in the restaurant, who suggested they have lunch before meeting his associate.

When they had placed their orders with the waitress, Rasheed got down to business. "Mr. Charlie," he said, "I'm not exactly a banker as I told you yesterday. Not in the traditional sense, that is. I am more of a facilitator. Through my connections I help people move money and raise capital for projects. Always very discreetly.

"The world is becoming a dangerous place for me and my kind," Rasheed continued. "There are so many new laws that I've decided to change my business. That is why I asked you to come today."

"Certainly Rasheed," Charlie replied, "but I don't understand enough of what you do and how you plan to change it."

Rasheed sighed. "I'm truly tired of the people I work with," he said. "I work very hard for too little return, and the types of deals are, to say the least, shady.

"I want to introduce you to these new people who own that yacht over there," Rasheed said, motioning to an eighty foot Hatteras. "You and I have the opportunity to manage their wealth. I will charge a management fee, and you will provide the offshore structures and banking facilities. This will permit me to move away from my old business and associates, and become a legitimate merchant banker such as yourself."

With that, Rasheed paid the check, and they walked down the pier to the yacht *Subterfuge*, where they were ushered into a large stateroom. Rasheed introduced Charlie to their host, John Hollow, and after several pleasantries which set a comfortable tone, the meeting began.

Paving the Way

Charlie started with his usual pitch about the offshore world and his business of forming offshore structures and international banking. He sensed that Hollow was slightly impatient, as if he had heard it all before, or perhaps he had been briefed by Rasheed. He didn't seem particularly interested in Charlie's credentials.

Then it was Hollow's turn. "I have an MBA in finance, and work for Señor Corazón," he said. "He has instructed me to invest a large sum of money for his three children where it will be safe."

"Would Mr. Corazón be our client," Charlie asked, "because the 'know your customer' rules require us to meet him, and get his passport and two letters of reference."

"I would be your client," Hollow replied. "Señor Corazón values his privacy. Rasheed and I have discussed his plan for managing the children's portfolio, and he has recommended you to handle the transactions, which will be sizeable."

"What would be the source of the funds we are to handle?" Charlie asked next.

"Señor Corazón made his money trading commodities with a country better known for its drug dealers," Hollow explained. "Because of high import duties, the trades were settled in cash, which has accumulated over the years."

"Excuse me," interrupted Charlie, "but we simply cannot accept cash."

"Nor will you," answered Hollow, unconcerned. "I have converted the cash through my own bank account, and will wire you the money."

"You are taking on a lot of responsibility," Charlie said. "If I were you, I would be worried about the source of this money. The days of being willfully blind are over."

"I know the money is legitimate," replied Hollow. "My concern is that the money be safe in your hands, since we will not go to court to get it back if you lose it. *Comprende?*"

"Well…" Charlie paused as the impact of this threat sank in, "there are no guarantees that investments always go up. Higher returns bring higher risks. Over time, with proper diversification, it has been shown that investing in the markets outperform fixed investments. But there can be losses along the way."

They concluded the meeting with Charlie promising to contact Rasheed tomorrow with his thoughts on how best to structure the Corazón children's portfolio.

That night, Charlie had a fitful sleep, half-dreaming, half-thinking about the meeting. The amount of money was tempting, and Hollow had covered the concern about source of funds; or had he? Charlie was no angel, but he was not about to accept a drug dealer into his clientele. Images of children selling drugs in schools and zombie-like addicts kept reappearing, disturbing his slumber.

On the other hand, Charlie could really use a client of this magnitude. How much trouble could he get into?

The Road to Hell

The next morning Charlie met Rasheed in their hotel for breakfast. "I'm sorry, Rasheed, but I've decided we cannot help you," he said painfully. "For three reasons: first, it's too dangerous; second, it's too dangerous; and third, it's too dangerous.

"First, it's too dangerous because this money is obviously proceeds of crime, exposing both of us to criminal sanctions for money laundering, quite probably jail," Charlie explained.

"Second, it's too dangerous because Señor Corazón will resort to violence if we lose any of his money," Charlie continued. "When it comes to investments, nobody is right all the time. An under-performing portfolio will be met with telephone threats or visits to your wife, or worse.

"Third, it's too dangerous because when this thing blows up, as it will, and if we survive the first two dangers, we won't be in business any longer," Charlie said. "The bad press and destruction of our reputations will ensure new careers for both of us, most likely selling shoes or used cars if not licence plates."

Rasheed was clearly disappointed, but seemed to take Charlie's advice in earnest, and the two men parted on friendly terms. Charlie returned to his room to find Victoria surrounded by bags and boxes, trying on the many fashions she had purchased in and around the resort.

Blinding Justice

Later that week, as Charlie and Victoria lined up for their flight home, Charlie was dreading the thought of enduring the new airport security procedures. He started to relax as they proceeded through the second stage of the gauntlet to the x-ray machine. Too soon: his carry-on bag was commandeered by the physical inspection person

"*Puedo reviser su equipage?*" asked a congenial face, not that Charlie had any choice if he wished to leave the country with his bag.

"*Esta bien*," Charlie replied, only to discover that the offensive item was a mahogany carving of a duck. The young lady carefully removed the bubble wrap, looked at the duck quizzically, and deferred to a large, muscular *hombre* of obvious authority looming behind her.

Without the slightest consideration, the *jefe* rattled off something in Spanish which Charlie's rudimentary Spanish could not decipher, but which likely meant the duck wasn't boarding the plane.

To illustrate his point, he then swung with his arm up and down, as if holding the *pato* as a weapon to smash the heads of the air crew.

"*El pato no esta permitido en el avion,*" stated the young woman sympathetically, as her boss strode off in search of another concealed threat to aviation.

Dumbfounded, Charlie could only reply: "*Este es un pato peligroso?*" He would not find justice here.

"*Si señor; no esta permitido,*" came the expected reply. Defeated, Charlie rewrapped his dangerous duck, returned to the start of the ticket queue, checked his carry-on bag, and began to re-run the gauntlet to his departure.

It was some months later Charlie learned that Rasheed had been arrested in one of the largest money laundering stings in history. About fifty people were detained in what was hailed as a great success which nabbed one of the Lex Luthor's of crime.

Rasheed was not the Lex Luthor in question, but it turned out he fell victim to substantial temptations put in his path by the undercover police running the sting. Despite Charlie's warnings, Rasheed took $500,000 in cash from Hollow, who told Rasheed it was drug money. All of the meetings on the yacht, which was owned by the police, had been videotaped. The thought police had Rasheed cold.

With nowhere to turn, Rasheed agreed to testify against his associates rather than risk the outcome of a jury trial. The judge gave him seven years in jail for his cooperation, which was half the sentence awarded to the so-called Lex Luthor.

The prosecutor inconveniently forgot his oral promise made to Rasheed to apply for a reduced sentence. After all, justice had been served: Rasheed's money and liberty were gone, and his reputation permanently destroyed, with seven years' incarceration to boot so he wouldn't even think about being tempted again.

Not surprisingly, Charlie was neither charged nor called as a witness, and his portion of the police tapes never surfaced. Like the dangerous duck, Charlie was safer in the checked luggage than on board with the passengers.

Epilogue

As Charlie relaxed in the steaming hot tub overlooking the beach and vast sea beyond, rum punch at hand, his mind recounted the events of the last eight years. He had been forced to switch banks more than once in order to stay in business, participated in the invasion of a sovereign country, tasted the state's hospitality twice, and almost got himself poisoned by a former client. He had to admit one thing: his life was hardly dull.

While Charlie was bouncing between events, the world was evolving in a direction that he found increasingly elusive. "The struggle underway between the big, high tax, high spend countries, and the smaller, no or low tax ones is now in full swing," Charlie said to nobody, since he was alone in the hot tub. "Ask anyone in international finance, and speculation on the very survival of the offshore jurisdictions quickly surfaces."

"The struggle for existence," as Charles Darwin called it.

A question on evolution posed by the comedian George Carlin came to mind: "If man is descended from apes and monkeys, why are there still apes and monkeys?" Charlie mused it was unlikely he meant politicians and bureaucrats in making this observation. "The ingenuity with which each side of the chase alternatively creates and undermines fiscal opportunities," he thought, "shows just how far they've both evolved."

For his part, Charlie was richer, wiser and more attuned to a world adrift in the crosscurrents of globalization, computerization and random violence.

Moving from the lonely hot tub to the cooler, more populated swimming pool, Charlie wondered where his unfolding world would take him next. As he accepted his two happy-hour cocktails from the grinning waiter, he was certain of one thing: the opportunities and challenges of his affairs were increasingly more unpredictable.

Some day he would have to retire to an out of the way island Paradise to relax and let the world pass him by. But that day had not yet arrived...

24.

Administratio Inexcusabilus

July, 2007

"Equipped to live in a world that no longer exists."

— Eric Hoffer

"The best thing I ever did," Walter Fulham QC was saying to Charlie over a glass of scotch in their favorite bar, The Happy Taxpayer, "was to hang up my shingle. I know it sounds crazy, but when you consider the myriad disadvantages of being a practicing lawyer, you will see what I mean."

"Except for the lawyer jokes," Charlie replied, looking at his glass as he swirled the scotch over the rocks, "most people I know would give their eye teeth to have a lawyer's status and standard of living."

"Understandably," said Fulham in earnest, "but they don't have to deal with all the red tape that the bar associations now wrap around you. Much like your complaints about intrusive governments bent on controlling your every move, the modern bar societies are ruled by bureaucrats who have little understanding of the realities most lawyers face. Consequently, their response to public criticism about lawyers is to pass regulations, the effect of which has been to raise the professional standard that a lawyer must meet to an unattainable level.

"When I started in law some forty years ago," Fulham continued, "we used to joke 'But for the Grace of God go I.' Now the joke has become a daily threat. It stares us in the face from the moment we awake. It hangs about us like a shroud, distancing us from our clients, sapping our will to give them the level of service they need."

"And so you don't stick your neck out for anybody, as Rick said in *Casablanca*," replied Charlie.

"Pretty much," said Fulham, as he ordered another round of drinks. "In my case, I can, since I no longer have the noseys looking over my shoulder; but the effect on the average lawyer has been to kill initiative and make them instruments of the state."

Signs of the Times

"Surely you are not saying we should expand the second great lie to apply to lawyers as well as civil servants," Charlie retorted with a laugh. "Not to mention doctors who toil for nationalized medical plans."

"Perhaps it is going too far to say you can't trust your lawyer," replied Fulham, "but there is no escaping the fact that you are not going to be well represented when your lawyer is worried that his advice and actions may be used against him later. Maybe even to take away his license to earn a living.

"Look, all I am saying is lawyers are human, with the same faults and frailties as everyone else," Fulham said. "They are now expected to be practically perfect in every way. As such, it is only a matter of time until they are burned by their governing body, unless they play it safe.

"The clients know this too. They now look at their lawyers as guarantors that everything will go right. When it doesn't, they expect the law society to pay from the insurance fund, which the law society is only too willing to do," concluded Fulham.

"I must admit I am having a little difficulty visualizing lawyers as Mary Poppins," Charlie said, amused by his old chum's turn of phrase. "But I take your point. If I were a lawyer, why would I do anything for my client that would jeopardize my career? It is another symptom of the eroding freedoms of modern society: everyone has to play by the rules.

"Oh for the days when the rules were few and far between," continued Charlie, "and it was the initiatives of the bold that were rewarded."

"Not anymore," replied Fulham. "Now the rewards are divided among the followers in ever tinier pieces."

"And so the meek shall inherit the earth," mused Charlie as visions of faceless people in brown suits loomed over him, killing his appetite for more alcohol.

"That is precisely why the underground economy continues to gain ground," added Fulham, "in spite of the ever more powerful tools that governments have to combat it. People are voting with their feet; doing what they can quietly to hold the peeping Toms at bay."

"If there were any doubt about the general concern about privacy," said Charlie, " all you need do is observe the proliferation of paper shredders at work and at home.

"Twenty years ago, I bought my first shredder for $800. There were three models to choose from, and it cross-cut the sheets five at a time," Charlie continued. "This year, I bought an equivalent model which cross-cuts up to ten sheets, as well as compact disks, at a cost of $169. I could choose from a dozen models.

"When I arrived at my office yesterday, I passed a large delivery truck from one of the office supply companies. It was

packed with paper shredders, and there were two men unloading them into the building next door. There had to have been 300 shredders in that truck. And the federal government is the only tenant in that building."

"I would surmise that the bureaucrats running their social programs," responded Fulham, "want to avoid prying eyes as much as their citizens do.

"Think about it: the citizen wants to keep as much of his property as he can, so he keeps quiet. But the bureaucrat stays equally quiet in order to avoid giving people knowledge which could be used to organize a revolt. The last thing rapacious governments want is an informed and unruly electorate," said Fulham.

"The shepherds cannot abide thoughtful sheep," replied Charlie, "for they may see them as wolves."

As the two friends went their separate ways, Charlie could not help but wonder what the future holds for individual liberty and the right to privacy when one of its key defenders, the legal profession, was well on its way to being a state-directed functionary.

"If history teaches us anything about economics," Charlie thought as he got behind the wheel of his vintage Mercedes sedan, "it is that economies thrive with free market capitalism and limited government regulation. Who is protecting us from the gradual erosion of freedom and initiative as we slide towards a new totalitarian state?"

Caution

Charlie had one stop to make before heading to the airport and his trip to points South to join Victoria. Her birthday was in two days, and Charlie had spotted a unique sculpture at a modern art gallery which he thought would strike her fancy. It was a stainless steel model of an old fashioned microphone, the kind used in the 1920's. Charlie knew it would make a great addition to Victoria's collection of movie memorabilia.

Arriving at Art Mode, an exclusive boutique which catered to the modern art set, Charlie went in to be greeted by an obsequious sales clerk.

"Ah yes, Mr. Smith," said the clerk with a frozen smile, "we have your item here. How would you like it wrapped?"

Charlie examined the sculpture. It stood about twenty inches tall on a round, cast iron base. At its top was a shiny stainless steel part filled with spongy plastic to resemble a microphone. Charlie's first thought was how it also resembled a grenade; his second was how would he transport it by commercial airliner to his island.

"Can we disassemble it, and wrap each part in bubble wrap?" asked Charlie. "Then I can put the pieces in my luggage, as I have to take them with me on an airplane."

Between them, Charlie and the clerk dismantled the sculpture into three pieces: the microphone, the twenty inch steel tube and the cast iron base. Then she carefully wrapped each, handing them to Charlie who placed them strategically in his suitcase that he had brought in from his car.

Bumps Ahead

Charlie arrived at the check-in counter one hour and eleven minutes before his scheduled departure. He presented himself and his papers at the first class desk, to be scolded by the clerk like a small child.

"Are you aware, sir, that your plane leaves in one hour?" she asked incredulously.

"I am," Charlie replied cautiously, instantly aware that he was in for a rough ride.

"Well, I am not sure they will let you on," the clerk continued, clearly beside herself with concern for Charlie's disregard for the rules. In her universe, people arrived from three hours (good) to two hours (acceptable) ahead of their departure time. Some even squeaked in one and one half hours (tolerable) ahead of time. Travelers simply did not arrive only one hour before their plane departed.

At this point she was on her phone to the gate. "You will?" she asked with panic in her voice. "Are you sure? Alright then, if you're ok with it".

She turned to Charlie with a look of disappointment. "The gate says you are allowed to proceed," she said sourly. "But in future you need to arrive at least two hours in advance to ensure you get on your flight. Sometimes the security inspection is very slow and the lines become long, and…"

"Thank you so very much," Charlie said quickly, cutting her lecture short, grabbed his tickets and left for the next station – the dreaded security lineup.

Slow Men Working

While Charlie negotiated his way through the crowded security bottleneck, watching all manner of security risks being removed and discarded (toothpaste, one inch pen knives, shampoos, bottled water and the like), his checked luggage was undergoing a rigorous inspection of its own.

"Come over here Elroy, I've got something you should see," said Aloicious with his characteristic slow speech.

"Hey man, what is it?" asked Elroy as he ambled over to the x-ray machine which displayed the contents of Charlie's suitcase.

"I dunno, but lookee here," replied Aloicious, pointing to three suspicious items. "Do you think we outta take a closer look?"

"Beats me," Elroy said. "You da x-ray man. You tell me."

The two security guards stood looking at the picture for some moments until Aloicious voiced his decision. "How 'bout we open the bag?" he asked without looking at Elroy, his eyes still transfixed by the picture.

"You da man," Elroy said again to give his buddy encouragement

The two men took Charlie's bag aside and opened it slowly, revealing its contents. Then Elroy put on rubber gloves and carefully unwrapped the three bubble-wrapped parcels, placing the three pieces of metal on the table for closer inspection.

"Are you thinkin' what I'm thinkin'?" asked Aloicious quietly.

"I'm thinkin' we'd best get the K9 patrol down here pronto," replied Elroy solemnly.

"But that'll take at least half an hour," said Aloicious. "No way this dude's bag'll arrive when he does."

"Not our problem," came Elroy's automatic reply. "We been told not to let nothin' suspicious onboard, and these here bomb pieces sure do look dangerous to me. We jest doin' our job."

Satisfied they were well within their mandate, the two men set the items and suitcase aside, called the K9 patrol, and waited.

No Thru Traffic

Some four hours later, the K9 squad arrived, which consisted of a policeman and a German shepherd trained to sniff out explosives.

"So boys, what you got for us this time?" asked Officer Trueblood, his dog Max in hand.

"Evenin' officer, how ya doin' Max," said Aloicious, motioning over to the offending pieces of metal. "We pretty sure we got ourselves some kind of bomb here."

Trueblood moved over to the table where his canine partner gave the items a cursory going over before turning away in search of something more interesting.

"Not according to Max," said Trueblood. "Have you tried to put them together to see what they look like? I can see by the threads they are meant to be screwed together."

"That's not our job, cap'n," replied Aloicious. "For that we need call our supervisor."

"Well, I suggest you do that," said Trueblood, "because somebody's going to miss their baggage."

"Too late for that," said Elroy with a chuckle. "This boy's done already arrive at his destination. He be lucky to get his stuff on the next flight out."

At that, Trueblood shrugged and led Max to their next assignment. They never seemed to have enough time to cover all the demands that came their way these days.

The supervisor eventually arrived, and the three of them cobbled the sculpture together by screwing the steel tube into the base at one end and the microphone shaped object at the other end. They even managed to get it standing upright on its base the first time.

"Looks like an old fashioned microphone," observed the supervisor, pleased with his handy work.

"Now that I see it all put together," said Aloicious, "I sorta see what you mean."

"I suggest you boys repack this bag, and sent it on its way," the supervisor said, and then added: "Oh, and by the way, good work. You can never be too careful. Know what I mean?" He patted Aloicious on his shoulder as he turned to leave.

"You bet," replied Aloicious with a big grin, motioning Elroy to repack the bag. Which he did, carefully, and then tossed it rudely onto the conveyor toward the next scheduled flight.

End of the Road

It did not take Charlie long to figure out what had happened to his bag, or why. He dutifully gave his particulars to an apologetic airline clerk, who predicted it would arrive on the next flight. She was close; it was delivered to Charlie within twenty-four hours.

Charlie was not overly polite to the clerk; in fact he was downright chilly, almost hissing comments through his teeth. From his point of view it amounted to a failure of service. He had entrusted his bag to the airline, which screwed up, again.

As Charlie stormed off towards the exit, the frustrated clerk turned to her co-worker and muttered: "I'd like to disconnect the lead to his pacemaker." From her point of view, the airline was caught between an irate customer and an airport security service on a mission.

A small inconvenience, to be sure. What was not lost on Charlie was how it evidenced a deteriorating system in need of repair.

"Oh well," sighed Charlie to Victoria, "until the world regains control of its priorities, if it ever does, we can expect to see increasing examples of this silliness."

"You should complain," offered Victoria sympathetically, knowing it to be a futile gesture.

"I very much doubt that would have any effect," Charlie

replied. "We can sit here and complain to our hearts' discontent about the lack of service, how nobody cares anymore, and so forth. And it's true; the old days have been replaced by the computer which is increasingly in charge, making its decisions dispassionately, expecting us to behave like automatons.

"My vote is to seek sanctuary wherever I can," Charlie continued. "How can those charged with digitizing the world ever appreciate the immortal words of Lord Byron:

'There is rapture in the lonely shore,
There is society where none intrudes.'"

"I'll drink to that," said Victoria, as she brought a ready '66 Latour, two crystal goblets and stinky cheeses.

25.

Atlas Shrunk

August, 2007

> *"Who knows what evil lurks in the hearts of men?"*
> — The Shadow

Nothing Charlie Smith ever experienced prepared him for what was about to happen.

He was sitting alone at a corner table set for two in the Bistro Restaurant near his office. It was a sweltering August day, and he was scanning the lunch menu pending his host's arrival.

Charlie had been summoned there anonymously by a note delivered to his receptionist that morning, which read:

> *I would be most grateful if you would dine with me at 12:30 p.m. today. The Bistro Restaurant is holding a reservation in your name. I trust the enclosed will ensure your attendance.*

The enclosure was a bank draft for $100,000 drawn on the Banque Internationale, an offshore bank known to Charlie. A sizeable sum to be sure, and one that normally brought a grateful tear to Charlie's eye.

In this case his heart skipped a beat as he noticed the payee on the draft. Instead of being Charlie's company, Global Wealth

Group, it was payable to Terranova Limited, an affiliated, offshore company whose existence was a closely guarded secret.

"How the hell do they know about Terranova?" Charlie thought as he examined the draft to determine if it was real.

"Miriam," Charlie called out to his receptionist, "am I free for lunch today?" She appeared moments later in his doorway, having printed the day's schedule from her computer.

"According to this," Miriam replied, "you have a 12:30 lunch appointment at the Bistro Restaurant, but is doesn't say who with."

Shaken

Sitting in the restaurant, Charlie felt a chill as he retrieved the note from his jacket pocket and read it again.

"*Bonjour*, Monsieur Smith," said a voice behind Charlie. He turned abruptly to see an impeccably dressed man in his mid-fifties with his hand outstretched in the universal gesture of goodwill.

As Charlie rose to take the hand, he barely recognized Jean-Philippe Couteau, an account executive from Banque Internationale that he had not seen in over six years.

"*Je m'excuse*," Couteau replied quietly as he looked furtively around the restaurant. "Shall we sit down?"

After the two men finished catching up and were tucked into their food, free from interference from the waiter, Couteau turned the conversation to the topic at hand.

"Please forgive the theatrics," Couteau began. "These are characteristic of our customer, who instructed the bank to find you. Are you familiar with the Club of Paris?"

Charlie shook his head slightly.

"The Banque Internationale has an important customer who has entrusted it with a locked case to be opened only in the event of his death," said Couteau. "If you are willing to accept the assignment, the case will be delivered to you."

"What is the assignment?" Charlie asked carefully.

"To safeguard the case and its contents," said Couteau.

"What's in the case?" asked Charlie.

"We do not know precisely, but we surmise it is information regarding the Club of Paris," answered Couteau. "All we have been told is the contents are highly sensitive."

"And the Club of Paris, what is that?" asked Charlie.

"The better question is, *who* is the Club of Paris," replied Couteau. "For two centuries there has been a group of influential people from Europe and latterly the Americas who control the world money supply.

"Many names you would recognize," Couteau continued. "They are highly placed in positions of power, and exercise influence on an incredible scale. It is their long-term plan to have the world run by a central government. They have the money; their focus is power."

As Charlie listened to the unfolding story, he kept thinking of the bumbler Malvolio in Shakespeare's *Twelfth Night* as he prepared to join those who "have greatness thrust upon them". Malvolio was set up, of course. Charlie was brought back to the discussion by Couteau's mention of the fee.

"The fee is yours to keep," Couteau was saying, "providing you accept the assignment. Specifically, you are to keep the case safe until its owner contacts you. In the event of his death, you are to call a number and follow the instructions you will receive."

"Am I to know the person's name?" Charlie asked

"He is an Englishman like you," replied Couteau, "by the name of Sir Arthur Girfelt. He is from a very old family, some say going back to the Knights of the Round Table.

"As a member of the Club of Paris, he is part of an organization intent on ruling the world. He has chosen you because you operate outside the system, disconnected from those in the positions of power."

"Very well, I accept," said Charlie, unsure if this was the best decision he had ever made. But the money was substantial, and he did not have much time for conspiracy theories.

With that, Couteau slid a leather attaché case under the table to Charlie. "You will find everything in here," Couteau said, as he handed Charlie a small key. "This ends the bank's involvement. It will disavow any knowledge of this affair if contacted by you or anyone else. *Au revoir*, Monsieur Smith, *et bonne chance*."

Without further discussion, Couteau walked away, leaving Charlie holding the bag.

Stirred

Back at the office, Charlie unlocked the attaché case to find an envelope and a small rosewood box about the size of a cigar box. It had a rotary dial lock with six numbered dials.

Inside the envelope was a card with a website address and a series of six numbers. "Not enough for a telephone number," Charlie thought. "Couteau must have meant that I access this website if Girfelt dies."

He next tried the numbers on the combination lock without success. "No harm in trying," Charlie consoled himself as he put the box on his bookcase amidst his rag tag collection of books. He put the envelope in a file folder marked "Paris", and had Miriam file it.

Charlie thought nothing more of the box, the envelope or the Club of Paris for six weeks. Then he received an email from an unknown source which told him to read an article on Arthur Girfelt at timesonline.co.uk.

Typing "girfelt" in the search box, Charlie found a one paragraph article about Sir Arthur Girfelt's untimely death. He had been found hanged in his London flat by the cleaning lady. Foul play was suspected.

After the shocking news had taken root, Charlie remembered his conversation with Couteau, and went in search of the Paris file.

With the card on his desk, Charlie navigated his computer to the website on the card, www.portal.co.uk. It was password protected. Then he entered the numbers from the card: 123456, but was denied passage.

"Obviously these numbers are the password," thought Charlie, "but in what order..." Not relishing the idea of trying every combination, he next tried them backwards, then odds and evens, and so forth, all without success.

Charlie stared at the computer screen, and the title *PORTAL* stared right back. Then it occurred to him to associate the numbers with the name. Rearranging the numbers in the same order as the letters produced the password 435612, and *voilà!* He was in.

Charlie was feeling pretty proud of himself when a virtual face appeared on the screen.

"Good morning, Mr. Smith," the face said. "I was Arthur Girfelt. As I am regrettably deceased, it is now time. Please open the box with the password you used to access this website."

The computer screen went blank, and Charlie turned his attention to the box lost amid the clutter of his bookcase. He dialed the numbers, and the lid flipped open to reveal ... nothing! He moved his fingers around inside the box to see if there were hidden compartments. Still nothing.

While Charlie sat slumped in his chair, contemplating this latest twist in a very unusual affair, Miriam came into his office.

"Excuse me," she said quietly with a puzzled look on her face, "there is a Mr. Girfelt in reception who says he is unexpected."

Straight Up

Sir Arthur Girfelt was a short, rotund man in his sixties, with a pudgy face and little, piggy eyes that gave nothing away. On one of his short, fat fingers was a large signet ring (with his family crest?). He wore a dark blue suit, white shirt, and red and blue striped tie (his military colors?). His presence exuded power.

Sitting across the boardroom table, Charlie thought this modern knight looked more like the fat man in *The Maltese Falcon*.

"Mr. Smith," Sir Arthur began. "We needed to be sure. I am pleased to say that you have passed the tests."

"I don't understand," Charlie replied in confusion.

"You followed Couteau's instructions to the letter," Girfelt said. "You did nothing until you were informed of my demise. If you accessed the website or opened the case earlier, we would have known. You also figured out the password. Your discipline and perseverance are qualities we value.

"Let me ask you a question: when is theft legal?" asked Girfelt.

"When the thief is the government, of course," Charlie replied.

"Precisely!" Sir Arthur guffawed, clearly ecstatic with this meeting of minds. Then he leaned forward, trying vainly to clasp his fat fingers together, his face deadly serious as he stared into Charlie's eyes.

"Now then, let's to business," he said.

"The Club of Rome exists to serve mankind and ensure its

future on this planet," Girfelt began. "This requires the centralizing of governments, in order to accomplish our goals on a global scale.

"In the past, protection from war was used by governments to control their citizens. Terrorism is the most recent version of this method. Through it, governments have been successful in curtailing a whole host of civil liberties. How can anyone argue in favor of terrorism?

"Going forward, with instant communication and a better informed electorate, we have selected the environment as the new threat to stabilize and integrate society.

"So far, we are pleased with the results," Girfelt continued. "People are accepting the rapidly increasing governmental intervention in their lives as a legitimate cost of survival. Most importantly, they are accepting the increasing taxation as necessary to save the planet. With more taxes comes more control, and control is necessary for a central world government to exist.

"At this point, you must be wondering about our interest in you," Girfelt said.

"The thought occurred to me," Charlie replied, transfixed by the scope of this man's reach.

"The offshore world, as you know it, is finished," Girfelt said. "Not today, or tomorrow, but soon. It is inevitable. As the great powers coordinate and tighten their control over the world, they will not tolerate opposition from states that are out of step.

"Your days are numbered, Mr. Smith, like it or not," Girfelt said with an air of finality. "You can join us, or be left behind."

Their meeting continued for an hour, and concluded with Charlie's promise to think about it. There was a lot to think about.

ISBN 1553953999-1

9 781553 953999